Knock Their Socks Off Marketing

Small Business Guide To Attracting More Customers In An Advertising Saturated World

J. WAYNE STORY

Published by Keystone Vortex Publishing, Rio Rancho, New Mexico

Story, J Wayne
    Knock Their Socks Off Marketing: Small business guide to attracting more customers in an advertising saturated world / J Wayne Story

ISBN 978-0-9889662-0-8

PRINTED IN THE UNITED STATES OF AMERICA

First Edition

Dedication

I would like to dedicate this book to the one person in my life who has done more to encourage me and help me be successful than anyone else, my wife, Linda.

She has always been the one who believed in me and pushed me to be better than I think I am. She did more to help us grow our three kids into loving, successful adults.

I have a tendency at times to be negative and she has always displayed a positive attitude and encouraged me to look on the bright side of each business challenge.

Without her encouragement and daily help I could not have written this book or created the businesses we have been privileged to own.

Table of Contents

INTRODUCTION

The SBA tells us that most new small businesses close the doors within the first 5 years of business. I've seen some numbers that indicate this is as high as 90%. That is appalling. I have made it my mission to improve that horrible statistic.

The SBA also tells us the most common reason that businesses close their doors is..."lack of sufficient working capital".

Let me interpret that reason for you. That is actually green eyeshade accountant speak for: "**not enough customers paying a sufficient amount of money for the product or service to create a profit large enough to sustain and grow the business.**"

When an entrepreneur starts his or her business, the farthest thing from the mind is planning to be out of business within 5 years.

The Problem? Most business owners start their business because he or she is really good at doing whatever product or service that business delivers.

He or she is really good at auto repair, or designing new dishes for the restaurant, or building houses, or creating business products, or....you fill in the blank.

Hardly any of the new business owners have training or skills in developing a marketing system to attract customers in sufficient numbers to sustain the business.

As a result, the business fails and the owner blames not having enough money to run the business until it is profitable.

The second BIG problem is the business owner's need to promote the business in an advertising saturated world. This is a world of advertising sameness where it is almost impossible to get your message noticed or heard.

This book is about helping business owners discover the marketing skills and systems that will cause their business to grow and flourish even during the toughest economic times and dull advertising overkill.

True small business success is more dependent on the owner's ability to attract customers and get a substantial price and profit for the product or service than on the product or service itself.

But few business owners understand this important axiom. Most think it is all about the product. For most of the rest of this book I will be using the generic "he" to refer to business owners and customers.

Please do not write me complaining about the lack of "she" in this book. I use the generic "he" for simplification alone. I have many coaching and consulting client business owners who are women. In fact, I have designed whole businesses to specifically concentrate on women customers in businesses that traditionally target men.

This book is about helping you, the business owner whether male or female, gain the marketing skills you need to get more customers giving you a sufficient profit to sustain your business for many years to come.

Chapter One

Knock Their Socks Off Marketing The Inspiration

I once stumbled on to an innovative small business entrepreneur with a big dream. This entrepreneur lived in a small resort town in Northern New Mexico where he cooked up this impossible dream. His Dream? Create a new local business, in an already crowded marketplace, with two primary competitors that were entrenched in the market for over 40 years and dominate that marketplace.

He had decided to birth a new real estate title company in a county dominated by resort, vacation and retirement properties and a mountain ski resort. Can you believe it? Small county, entrenched competitors, new start-up business with no existing customers, and unique property types, nevertheless our entrepreneur was undaunted.

He was convinced he could accomplish HIS goal to dominate the real estate closings in his county and the adjacent counties within 3 years. Sounds like a "fool's errand" doesn't it? It is for 99.8% of entrepreneurs starting a brand new business. But this guy possessed three assets that few business owners have, or develop when they first start in business.

- ✓ He knew how to launch "Massive Marketing Action."
- ✓ He knew how to get off the "Boring Train."
- ✓ And, he confidently crafted a marketing plan to **"Knock the Socks Off His Prospects."**

Would you like to know the result of his taking "massive marketing action"? In less than two years, he gobbled up over 51% of all real estate title transactions in the county.

I repeat...in **less than** two years!

How would you like to command more than 51% of your competitive market? Hang with me through this book and I'll reveal many of the insider strategies 1 use to accomplish that for local bricks and mortar business owners over and over again.

Grab <u>YOU</u> Some
"Non-Traditional" Marketing

Our New Mexico entrepreneur chose to use what I call "Non-Traditional" Marketing. (We will call our entrepreneur "Marvin" just to protect the embarrassment of his competitors.)

2

Instead of investing all his time and budget on "Brand Advertising", Marvin launched a non-traditional advertising campaign aimed directly at his target market.

You know what I mean by "brand advertising". That is the main strategy taught by most in the advertising business. Advertising agencies, graphic designers and media sales people will advise you to invest a lot of your hard-earned money and time in:

- choosing just the right corporate name,
- designing a memorable logo,
- crafting a 4-6 word catchy phrase (byline) that describes your business,
- creating elegant, professional letterhead, envelopes, and business cards,
- And, advertising that name and logo for months and years until the market becomes so familiar with it that they always remember you.

But that WAS NOT where our smart marketer started with his business!

First, he identified a significant hole in the marketing strategies of his competitors. Give me a significant <u>hole</u> and I'll beat anyone, even with the best brand in the business.

There were no compelling reasons for a real estate or home buyer to use one competitor over the other. Truthfully, his competitors were devoid of any true marketing strategy.

Marvin's entrenched competitors depended on the fact that they had been in the market for SO long, everyone just HAD to choose them.

The only competitive advantage these "stuck in the mud" title companies had was tradition. Everyone just "traditionally" put the existing title companies on the real estate contract out of habit, no more no less.

Here lay Marvin's biggest dilemma. You have probably experienced this if you've sold a house in the past few years. The title company you employed in a real estate transaction was almost always determined by the real estate agent handling the sale for you. Or, sometimes a mortgage loan consultant or banker made the recommendation if the buyer and seller were entering a contract without an agent.

AND, all these "influencers" in Marvin's area had developed a habit of using the same title company for years, kind of like pulling on an old comfortable pair of socks. To change those habits, he would have to "Knock Their Socks Off" to get their recommendation during the purchase contract writing process. Our new title company owner decided he would design a company that solved problems.

First, he identified the key "dissatisfiers" for real estate agents. The local real estate agent was his target prospect, since most of the time THEY decided what title company to use in a real estate purchase. Marvin immediately set in place his "massive action plan." He started with a multi-step multi-media "Knock Their Socks Off" marketing campaign to blast his company into this difficult marketplace. Right off the bat, the second letter sent out introducing his company included a pair of socks and a two page sale letter enclosed in a large white envelope.

The headline on the letter inside?

Our Services Will Knock Your Socks Off, That's Why We're Sending You These Replacements

You see he took "Action." He didn't wait to gently move into the market place. He jumped off the "Boring Train" that every other business in his area was following. AND, he "Knocked The Socks Off" his prospects right out of the gate.

His entrance into this closed marketplace did not include <u>JUST</u> an announcement or two that he was open for business as you see from most business start-ups. His marketing plan featured a total of 16 individual marketing steps including:

- direct mail letters,
- CD players with CD ready to play introducing his business,
- bag with a candy bar,
- envelope with a silver platter,
- miniature trash can mailer, and
- telephone calls.

All this....accomplished in the first 12 weeks of opening business – Massive Action.

What were the results? Within the first two years he claimed over 51% of all real estate title work in the county. And the other two entrenched title companies? They were left wondering. . . . "What Happened?" and had to settle for splitting what was left.

There is another lesson here you should not miss

Marvin WOULD NOT accept that he had to slowly work his way into the market. He knew that aggressive, creative, smart "non-traditional" marketing was the answer to growing a business exponentially in almost any business environment.

My purpose in sharing this book with you is to demonstrate how you can use the three primary action steps he employed to skyrocket your business success with smart, prospect engaged marketing.

What were they again?

✓ Get off the "Boring Train"
✓ Craft a marketing plan to **"Knock the Socks Off Your Prospects"**
✓ Launch "Massive Marketing Action."

I will be your guide down the sparsely traveled trail of strategies I use in client businesses to get attention in their marketplace and grow their business faster than any other business in whatever industry they have chosen.

Would you like to do that in your industry? You can! It just takes action, a change in advertising method, and smart "Knock Their Socks Off Marketing".

Chapter Two

Stop Doing and Start Marketing

B efore I begin sharing with you how to implement "Knock Their Socks Off Marketing" in
your business, we must first address an un-
comfortable discovery I made as a small
business owner.

As I developed my first $1+ Million a year website
catalog company, which I started back in the early
days of the internet, I had a revelation.

"I must learn to be the marketer of my company."
As a small business owner, I MUST NOT relegate that
responsibility to someone else.

I CAN assign marketing tasks that I design to
someone else, but the marketing plan, the marketing
message, the hole to fill in the marketplace, must

come from the business owner....the driving force of the business.

As I started Santa Fe Décor Inc, back in 1999, I identified a hole in the marketplace and decided to fill it using a non-traditional method.

My wife, Linda, and I were living in Houston, Texas at the time. Yes, I'm a born-and-bred Texan and proud of it. But please, don't hold that against me.

We were traveling throughout the Southwest (New Mexico and Arizona) and Linda had fallen in love with the simplistic beauty and design of southwest style homes and decor.

We started accumulating Southwestern style decorating pieces for our home as we traveled. She was determined to change the boring decorating style of our home back in Houston.

It would be different from the same old interior decor everyone else was using. BUT, we had a problem. There was only one dumpy little store in Houston that carried any of the designs we wanted and their choices were s-o-o-o limited.

When Linda wanted to change over the design of a room, we had to wait until we traveled back out to the Southwest on vacation. But that was a slow process over several years.

In fact, on several trips, we drove our van 16 hours; all the way from Houston to Santa Fe (instead of a short airline flight) just to pick up the bigger items Linda wanted.

As we were driving back from one of these long arduous trips, it hit me. Duh! I'll bet other people in the country have the same problem, but live even farther away and don't have time to travel out to Santa Fe as often.

Then Linda and I started to scheme a new business idea. We would offer southwest style décor for the home in a mail order catalog with photos of all the beautiful Southwestern home décor we had found.

There Was One BIG Problem

Choosing just the right designs and producing a printed catalog was very expensive and fraught with small business land mines.

For several years, I had used the internet to market several products I was selling in my invention marketing company, UltraTech Products Inc. The web was in its infancy at that time – mid-1990's.

It dawned on me one day.

We could test what people wanted (and would buy) from a mail order company much easier, if we created a virtual catalog – on this new internet website thing.

It worked so well, that we built that company into the largest Southwestern and Western style home décor website in the country in just 3 years.

Drive the Competitors
Out of Business

In fact, we ultimately drove three printed southwestern décor catalogs out of the business using the internet as our catalog media.

We could bring new designs to market faster while testing to determine what the marketplace really wanted. This was significantly easier and more cost effective than was ever available through a printed catalog.

When we started the company, I was doing everything, as we all usually do when we start a new enterprise.

I was teaching myself web design, search engine optimization, product photography, graphic design, packaging, shipping and just about everything else.

Because it all depended on me, there was a growth capacity problem. I was just struggling to get a decent income out of the business.

What Business Are You In

Even as we started adding employees, I was still spending most of my time working in the business. Then one day I was in a conference with one of my small business growth mentors, Dan Kennedy. He asked "what business are you in." I explained that I was in the website catalog business.

Then he had the audacity to challenge my business owner manhood. He calmly announced to the whole room, "You are wrong." How could that be? EXCUSE ME? I knew what business I was in better than he did.

Then came one of the biggest ah-ha moments of my small business life. He explained that I **WAS NOT** in the website catalog business. I **WAS** in the business of "MARKETING my website catalog products".

That was an "earthquake opens up the earth and I fell in" moment. I grappled with that mind twist for several gut wrenching days. I know, I know....I am a little slow. Then that message dropped on me like a ton of bricks.

He was right. As long as I invested all my time in running the catalog business, we were going to struggle. That is when I realized as a small business owner, I HAD to be in the Marketing Business.

Most Important Job
Marketing Your Business

So your first big decision, in adopting and using "Knock Their Socks Off Marketing", is to ensure you are working on **"Marketing Your Business"**, 20 – 30 – 40% or more of your business month.

As Dan Kennedy would say it, you must be "working ON your business not just IN your business." That is your first pivot point to exponential growth of your business.

As a friend of mine is fond of saying, "that's a writer-downer".

I am the first to admit, this will be difficult at first. After I made the decision to change, it was difficult for me to find the time. It would have been so much easier to hire someone else to do marketing. But the results would have been sketchy at best. In fact, I tried that. I bought advertising and had the media salesperson help me find someone to design the message and the ad copy. That failed miserably.

However, the more I donned the title of *Marketer of My Business* and studied small business marketing, the faster our business grew. I discovered that every time I added a marketing step, the business grew and I could afford to add an employee to take some of the "in the business" work off my back.

Employees Added 50%+ Growth

I found that every time I added an employee that took some of the day-to-day grind off my back, the business grew by 50% or more. That would not have happened though, if I was not learning and creating marketing systems for the business.

One of my clients, Steve, owns an auto repair shop in Albuquerque. He also learned this "in the business of marketing his business" the hard way.

For a number of years, he was the primary employee in his auto repair shop. In his best years, he was creating about $350,000 a year in total sales.

That is actually pretty good for the average auto repair shop. But like most of us, he was doing everything. He was the service writer, the bookkeeper, mechanic, parts order specialist, everything.

After expenses his meager income meant he was just scraping by. Then one day he discovered "Knock Their Socks Off" style marketing and realized he needed to stop doing all the work.

He started studying and using our type of direct response marketing for his business. He started working *"on his business"* as well as *"in his business"*.

His meager little auto repair shop business started to grow. And, the business became fun again. As a result, he grew his business to revenues of more than $1.2 Million a year......in just 3 years.

Real Small Business Entrepreneurs

If you are a true small business entrepreneur, you will find that after about a year or two of just doing the business, it becomes boring. It starts to be an anchor and chain to your creativity.

But someone has to do the work, right? Change your role to Director of Marketing and Director of Business Design and it becomes fun again.

Now Steve spends about 2 1/2 days a week in the shop. Every Wednesday he takes the whole day off to go play golf. When he discovered his days in the shop had to be dedicated to attracting more customers and managing employees, not repairing cars, the business grew by over 300% in just the next three years.

You can do the same. But what do you think is the most important asset you need in your business in order to accomplish this? I want you to stop reading, sit in a moment of silence, and ponder your answer.

STOP, don't peek yet. What do you think it is?

You need
- a steady flow of warm prospects,
- prospects turning into customers AND
- more sales from existing customers.

Stop Being Your Employee And Be An Entrepreneur

To make this "Marketing-centric" transition in your business will require an EXTRORDINARY effort for a short time. That is why we are entrepreneurs. We understand a significant investment in time NOW means more free time doing what we want and higher income in the future.

Isn't that what makes the difference between Employees and Entrepreneurs? Ask yourself, are all business owners Entrepreneurs?

No, many small business owners have just traded an employee job for being an employee of a company they own. If you are now Self-Employed, you may still JUST be an employee. It is just that now YOU are responsible for all the company daily operations, reporting, books, taxes, etc. etc, etc.

What turns you into an entrepreneur instead of a self-employed job owner?

I am sure most of you are familiar with Robert Kiyosaki, the author of the book "Rich Dad Poor Dad".

If not you should go read that book. It will change your perception of what you should be emphasizing in your business.

Kiyosaki calls this....creating wealth by understanding the cash flow quadrant.

Robert Kiyosaki's Cash Flow Quadrant	
Employee	**Business Owner**
# E	# B
You Have a Job	You Own a System & People Work For You
Self Employed	**Investor**
# S	# I
You Own a Job	Money Works for You

In his first book, Kiyosaki tells us, if we want our business to make us wealthy, we must move from Self-Employed to Business Owner. Then we must take the cash thrown off by our business activities and move to Investor. That's where the big wealth is created. So what is the difference between employee and Business Owner Entrepreneur? It is the implementation of *"working ON your business rather than always working IN your business"*. It is also the understanding of urgency and massive action.

Chapter Three

Massive Action Beats Slow and Steady

T he purpose I had in starting you off with Marvin's story was to encourage you, as a business owner, not to accept slow and steady as a business model.

Many in your industry will suggest THAT is the best plan for you. But the truth is, that is the plan THEY chose and — it is painful. They did it that way. And, they want you to suffer through it the same way they did.

Your competitors developed their businesses slow and steady. So they want you to plod along through the same agonizingly slow growth they did. AND, that way you won't be a competitive threat to them for quite a while.

You need to be smarter than that.

In most cases the only difference between you and Marvin's massive growth is to stop accepting "slow and steady" as a marketing business plan and just take "massive action".

But HOW?

One of the signs of a true entrepreneur is that he or she never accepts things the way they are. That is what employees do. Do you have an employee mindset or an entrepreneur mindset?

Testing My Entrepreneur Mindset

Several years ago, I decided to test the waters of commercial property ownership.

I knew I had a lot to learn so I decided to start by building a new corporate headquarters for the four companies I owned at the time.

One of my companies was already investing in residential real estate so I already had some basics of property investment. I decided this would be a great learning experience.

AND Man WAS IT EVER A "LEARNING EXPERIENCE"!

Who says the government is here to help you?

I spent an enormous number of hours and numerous delays working with the general contractor and the city where we live to get our new 15,000 sq. ft. headquarters building project completed.

I worked with the city to get approval for the project, approval for the building design and approval for each step of the construction process.

I had FINALLY made it through all of the city red tape and we were getting down to the final occupancy permit inspections and move in date.

I had given our existing landlord 60 days notice that we were ending our lease and moving out at the end of February.

All of a sudden, just a few days away from our move out deadline, the fire inspector found a problem with our building's fire sprinkler system. It seems, no one designed in or installed a shut-off valve between the city water supply and our sprinkler supply system in the ground outside the building.

There was a shut-off valve inside the building, but n-o-o-o that wasn't enough.

Never mind that the sprinkler system had already been approved and no one required it. Never mind that the city inspector's office had approved the plans and had never noted that one was required. Never mind that the new rule requiring this small detail had been instituted by the city about 6 months after we had our plan approvals and started construction.

We are now five days away from having to be out of our lease space and the construction company personnel are shaking their heads and saying "it just can't be done in such a short interval".

Well Wayne's "entrepreneur mindset" sense of urgency and massive action gene kicked in. I was not going to accept that this just couldn't be fixed and we could not move in on the first of March. We had to be out of our building. The landlord was demanding the space back.

I COULD NOT afford to shut down the business until this was fixed and could get the City Inspector's permission to move into our new building.

I knew customers would be calling on Monday morning and we weren't going to have any offices or phones. Can you feel my frustration?

The construction company told me there were just too many hurdles to overcome.

- First, the valve we needed had to be installed 12 feet down in the ground on the city side of the water supply.
- Second, that valve was very large and none were available in the state.
- Third, once we opened up the water supply to install the valve, the city would require a new inspection of the water system by a different inspector from the city water department.
- Fourth, after he approved the valve installation, we had to close up the 12 foot deep hole.
- Then we had to order an independent testing lab to come out, collect water samples and test them in a lab to make sure we had not contaminated THE CITY WATER SUPPLY.
- Are you hearing my frustration yet?
- Fifth, the city fire inspector would have to come back out and complete the final fire inspection.
- Sixth, we would THEN have to have the city's final occupancy inspection completed (by a different inspector) to get our permit allowing us to move into the building.

According to the construction company, that was an impossible task in just 5 days. AND, we had already lost half a day talking about it.

I just couldn't accept this hypothesis. I explained to the construction company we WOULD get this DONE!

My "Massive Action" entrepreneur gene kicked in. I kicked the contractor into gear and had him call around the country to secure a valve and have it air shipped into town overnight, first problem solved. At the same time I had the construction company start digging the 12 foot deep hole in the ground to be ready as soon as the valve arrived. The valve was installed on day two.

Next big problem: you can't schedule a city inspector until all work is actually completed. When you call the inspection department, they put it on their schedule and if they are not t-o-o busy, they may send the inspector out in the next day or two...maybe.

Well that just would not work for me.

Wayne's Rule
You Must Stop Accepting Others' Limitations

I called the city planning department manager that was responsible for the permit and inspection departments and scheduled an urgent meeting the next morning.

I related all the delays the City permit departments had caused over the last 10 months of getting a building completed that should have only taken 5 months of construction.

I explained I had to move out of my existing lease and the city would stop getting tax revenue during the time I couldn't accept orders. I also explained (gently) that I would make sure the mayor knew about the loss in revenue.

He agreed to help and told his department managers to complete our inspections within an hour or two after we called them, next problem solved.

Now the last big hurdle was "water testing".

The construction company called the testing lab and was told the lab technician would be glad to get out and do the test in a couple of days.

A COUPLE OF DAYS? I couldn't wait a couple of days. The construction company employee said that was all we could do. "You just couldn't rush these guys. They would slow down even more if we did", he said.

Massive action kicked in again. I got on the internet and did some research to find out the name of the president of the testing company. I called his office and booked a face to face appointment that afternoon. After explaining my dilemma, he agreed to send out one of his lab techs that next morning to collect the samples.

By 1:00 PM, we still had not received a report from the lab. So, I drove back over to the lab and asked for the lab supervisor. He patiently explained to me that the lab work just takes time. But, I didn't have time. It was 1:30 on Friday, the last day of the month. I had inspectors waiting for us to call. I (politely) explained I would wait in the lobby until they completed the test. AND, they might have a hard time explaining to the employees and customers why there is a "raving lunatic" pacing back and forth in the lobby. Ten minutes later the lab report magically appeared. So much for: "lab work just takes time".

I jumped in the car and raced back across town while at the same time calling the city fire inspectors and the city final occupancy inspectors to get them out to the construction site, RIGHT NOW.

At 4:17 that Friday afternoon just 4 ½ days later, we received our final occupancy certificate.

Our staff was already poised with moving trucks, packed and ready to move. We started immediately and moved 5,000 square feet of office systems, warehouse shelving, inventory, packaging and shipping equipment and were live taking orders on Monday morning.

It was not perfect. But, the business was live and operational. Our customers could not tell the difference. I just would not take normal for an answer when the whole business and our customers were depending on getting this problem fixed.

Massive Action Means
Not Accepting Normal

Massive action means not accepting that something cannot be done in a short time frame. Massive action means creating urgency to get it done in the shortest time possible.

The construction company employees told me that in all their years, they had never seen a task as impossible as this one accomplished in such a short unreasonable amount of time.

But you CAN accomplish similar feats, with the right motivation, a sense of urgency and MASSIVE ACTION! Massive action is not only defined by taking action on a problem, but also in implementing your plans for marketing and selling your products and services.

But Massive Action in Marketing May Cause Mistakes and Cost Lots of Money, Right?

You are probably concerned about making mistakes that cost you thousands of dollars in advertising if you take massive action and hurry the project, right?

But what isn't obvious as the pimple on a beautiful girls face is the advertising you are doing now is most likely costing you those same thousands of dollars without results. AND, you are missing customers and prospects you could have attracted already.

I invest most of my time these days helping other small business owners get exponential growth in their business with direct response marketing and advertising strategies.

I also host my Small Business Marketing Power-Circle™, a monthly meeting of 60 - 80 small business owners studying and using these types of strategies in Albuquerque, New Mexico.

Quick Income Boost Needed

One day a couple of years ago, I needed a quick income boost for my marketing consulting company, Direct Marketing Strategies Rx Ltd.

I knew that a number of our PowerCircle™ members were struggling with the basic concepts of the strategies I was sharing with them each month. They could see they needed to use these strategies but just didn't know how to implement.

My need and their need merged into a new seminar product for my business: **"11 Insider Secret Steps to Growing Your Business More in the Next Year Than Ever Before."**

This was a full day seminar covering all the basics that had grown my businesses exponentially. Once I made the decision to hold the full-day seminar, **my massive action kicked in** and I completed:
- ✓ All the marketing items,
- ✓ 2 direct mail letters,
- ✓ A postcard,
- ✓ Two emails and
- ✓ The complete course in just 10 days.

Most business owners would have taken weeks or even months for a similar task. They might do a study with interviews to see what people wanted. Then they would solicit opinions about which day of the week and what month to hold it.

Next, they would start researching just the right advertising method to use to attract seminar participants, etc. etc.

Maybe in 6 months they might pull it all together.

Massive Marketing Action

I decided I couldn't wait that long. I set a goal for myself to have the seminar all ready to go in 2 weeks. **I beat my deadline with room to spare.**
- I negotiated with the hotel,
- Set the date,
- Developed sales letters, postcards and emails to get sales,
- Obtained a mailing list of my target audience,
- Developed email follow-ups,
- Wrote scripts for telephone follow-ups, and
- Created the outline and scripts for the workshop.

All that in just 10 days while keeping the rest of my business operating.

I received a good sized payday. Participants invested $297 each for my one-day seminar and I filled the hotel conference room. And, the participants received a massive amount of information they could use immediately to grow their business.

Everyone won!

I would have missed significant client satisfaction. I would have missed several consulting clients that came as a result of the workshop training. I would have delayed the income my business needed right then, without Massive Action.

Massive Action Is Not
Hiring an Ad Agency

So what kind of "massive action" am I talking about when it comes to marketing? Let me explain a little further.

First off, "massive marketing action" is not spending vast amounts of your hard earned dollars hiring an advertising agency to advertise for you in the yellow pages, magazines, trade periodicals, newspapers, and TV or radio. As a small business owner, you MUST be in control of your marketing message yourself. You do not want to turn that over to some third party advertising agency.

I am talking about YOU taking control. You must of course study and learn "Knock Their Socks Off" low cost marketing systems that you can implement yourself. In fact, you will find these to be significantly more effective. Advertising agencies may work well for large lumbering multi-national corporations, but not for the average small business owner like you.

First, let's look at how most advertising agencies earn their money. You contract with them to create some advertising for you. They come up with several creative ideas and you get to choose one. Then the advertising agency goes out and secures media buys to run your advertising that both you and the agency have agreed upon.

Did you know that most of an ad agency's income is created in these media buys? It usually sounds good to the business owner because they do not have to pay for the creativity of the Advertising Agency staff.

What's The Motivation For the Advertising Agency?

For several years, I owned part interest in a Mobile Billboard advertising media company. When we sold an advertising campaign using our mobile billboard trucks to an advertising agency, we were required to kick back 15% of the contract to the agency as compensation for bringing us the customer.

Think about this for a minute. You have hired an advertising agency whose primary income comes from how much media they can get you to buy. Where do you think their loyalties lie, getting you results at the lowest cost? Or, is it getting you to buy as much media as possible.

In fact, this is where the concept of branding came into being. If you choose branding as your advertising plan, you have to spend a whole lot more on advertising media.

Brand Advertising vs. Direct Response Advertising

AND, who comes out ahead in a long branding campaign? The ad agency does. That is not the case with direct response advertising.

In direct response advertising, I will know exactly what the return is on every marketing dollar spent. I want to know if I spend $1,000 will I get $5,000 or $10,000 or more dollars of business. I want to be able to tie the results directly to whatever marketing system I am using. Now don't get me wrong. I'm not painting the whole advertising agency business with this same wide brush......just most of it.

There are a few ad agencies that specialize in direct response advertising and do build a specific reporting system into the advertising pieces and media used. They are just hard to find. If you decide to hire an agency that is the kind you need to find.

IF, you hire an advertising agency, your first question should sound something like this. "What kind of tracking mechanism will you employ so I can know exactly how much business your advertising brings in?" If the ad agency Account Executive hem-haws around and doesn't have a quick, good answer, run like the devil is after you. That agency is more interested in winning awards and getting you to buy more media than in getting results.

No Tracking – No Marketing Plan

Before I start breaking down Massive Marketing Action, I must start by explaining that all of the marketing I create is designed to immediately chronicle exactly what response rate we are getting from our marketing.

I want to know the return on investment (ROI).

You must know:

- How many leads your marketing actions produce?
- How many sales did those leads produce?

- **And, more importantly,** what is the lifetime value those new customers contribute to your business?

Right now, before you start anything else, I advocate for all of my clients the following Wayne's Rule.

Wayne's Rule
No Known Lifetime Customer Value, No Valid Marketing Plan

You must calculate, for your business, what an average new customer delivers in sales over the next year, two years, five years and lifetime value. This number does not have to be perfect, but you need a general idea of what value they bring to your business.

Without that information, you can never calculate how much you ought to invest in advertising and marketing to get that prospect added to your customer list. You will be shooting in the dark with your marketing. What happens when you shoot in the dark? You expend all your ammo and IF you hit something it is almost always the wrong person.

So your first assignment in "Knock Their Socks Off Marketing" is to calculate "lifetime customer value" (LCV) for your customer base. This requires some research in your business.

With the LCV number in hand, it will be far easier to make decisions about your marketing investments. Understanding your LCV will also give you the motivation to create a system that acquires those new customers more systematically.

Chapter Four

You've Chosen Massive Action, Now What?

Okay, let's get started. You made the first and most important decision. You have decided to become the *"Marketer of Your Business"* - rather than – *"Doer of Your Business"*.

To make this transition will require an "Extraordinary Effort" for the next few months, maybe even up to a year. That is why we are entrepreneurs.

That's what makes the difference between Employees and Entrepreneurs. It is the extra effort we are willing to invest for the first few years to establish a business with significant value.

Now then, you have decided to be the Marketer of your business and create massive action with super-human effort (at least by our employee's standards).

So, where do you start?

First, you must answer the most important question about your business: #1 Question, Numero Uno, the "you know it or else" question.

Top of the Heap Action Question

Why should a prospect, or your current customer, take a chance on doing business with you despite all of the other choices they have to spend their money?

You must answer this in a way that will be significantly meaningful for your marketplace, prospects and customers.

Here is your First Exercise. Write the above statement at the top of a sheet of paper and list the reasons.

So how do you come up with the answer?

First you need to define and understand your prospect's needs, wants and emotional triggers. If you can define your business around their needs, wants and emotions in a unique way, you get the win.

Dan Kennedy is fond of telling the story of two guys that reopened a failing pizza restaurant near a college campus.

The restaurant continued losing money and one of the partners bailed out of the business. Have you ever had that experience?

The one left behind changed his business from an eat-in, come to us, failing business model to one of the largest pizza franchise companies in the country. He did it all with a simple 9 word answer to this #1 Question.

Fresh Hot Pizza in 30 Minutes or Less, Guaranteed

Of course I am talking about Tom Monaghan and Domino's Pizza. Let's analyze what he did. First he figured out that his biggest prospect base was the college student at the local University stuck in his or her dorm room or house studying.....every waking moment.

Tom knew they often came in and ordered takeout pizza but it was frequently cold by the time they remembered to come pick it up and take it home. So he promised it would be "Fresh and Hot." He didn't promise the best pizza or even good pizza by the way. (Words like best and great pizza would have been meaningless because they deliver no graphic image to the brain that causes action.)

But in the beginning, Tom's customer didn't care that it wasn't the best quality pizza in the world. Tom knew all they cared about was that it be hot and quick. He also added a meaningful and measurable guarantee. 30 Minutes or it's free. I will get to the importance of guarantees in another chapter. He was taking advantage of our natural competitive nature. The customer was competing with the delivery guy to see if a FREE pizza was in the offing when it was delivered in 31 minutes instead.

Few of us are able to (in just 9-15 words) create such a strong USP (Unique Selling Proposition sometimes called an Elevator Speech). But it is a critical exercise, even if it takes a paragraph or two.

Answer the question, "Why are you truly different?" You MUST forge a plan for taking yourself out of the commodity business. You do that by having a truly "Unique Selling Proposition".

I told you earlier about my website catalog company, Santa Fe Décor Inc. When I started the company back in 1999, I made some assumptions because I didn't know any better. I assumed that because we were on the internet, we had to compete with the other websites on price and price alone. When a prospect came to the Web to find a product they wanted, they could easily price shop with every other site on the WEB. That makes sense unless you know what we know now.

In the retail industry there is an industry norm. Retail price in stores for most items is set at what is called "Keystone". That is 100% mark-up from the wholesale price the manufacturer charges.

Since we were on the internet, we decided it needed to be less than that and set our price at 85% mark-up. After all, people on the Web could easily go from site to site and compare prices.

Many of the products we carried were the same products offered by other websites. So, what else could we do? We had to keep the price lower, right? We would regularly check our primary competitors on the web and set our price just a little under their price.

The problem with this pricing model is that it made our margins very, very thin. But, we figured that since we didn't have as much overhead as a retail store, we could sell for less. However, a "big boulder in the road" problem remained, low margins meant low profits.

After studying non-traditional marketing for several years, I decided to test a new pricing structure. I raised all our prices to 120 – 150% of our wholesale price.

They Could Not Believe What I Did

Everyone around me was flabbergasted. The competitors couldn't believe it. In fact, I'm sure they were smiling behind their hand. They were thinking, "this dummy has blown it and we'll get all his business". The truth is they did get some of our business. In fact they were the beneficiaries of about 10% of our customers.

STOP! Did you notice that? I just told you I gave away 10% of my customers.

But what my competitors didn't know? Raising my prices and giving away 10% of my customers actually increased my total profit......overnight......109%. Oh, and the customers that left me for my competitors were the ones who only bought on price, were the biggest complainers and more frequently returned product. I WON!

I more than doubled my profit with this move. But how could I accomplish such a feat. Wouldn't the prospects searching the Web just go some place where it was cheaper? Actually they will not, IF you have sufficiently answered the "top of the heap" question I gave you at the beginning of this chapter. Our company had some amazing advantages going for it that weren't apparent to our competitors.

First, we had worked diligently getting our website at the top of the search engine pages for all of the words people usually used to search for our type products.

There is a funny perception when people search the web for products to buy. If the searcher finds a particular business in the first or second position for every search phrase he types, he immediately assumes that company is somehow more reliable and better. That is a fallacy, but understanding how your customer thinks and makes decisions is vitally important to your success.

Second, we had live design consultants the customer could ACTUALLY call, talk to, and get help from when deciding what to order. The prospect didn't have to put up with voice mail like they did with most of our competitors.

The customer was often looking for someone to confirm they were making the right decision. In fact, many times our customer would ask us which design we thought she ought to order.

You see most internet business owners believe incorrectly that the customer comes to the internet so they don't have to deal with a salesperson.

Some probably do. But most are like any other customer in your life, they want someone to make recommendations and help them make a decision.

We provided a live person on the telephone to help the prospect or customer. Most of my competitors tried to avoid talking to customers by hiding behind a website and voicemail.

Our competitors didn't know it, but they were missing a lot of business and it stuck them having to compete by price.

Third, we had designed the website in a very different way that made it easier for our customer to view and understand.

Fourth, we offered fabric samples the customer could hold, touch and feel. Fabric samples? Seems insignificant doesn't it? But it solved a big issue for women ordering fabric design products through the web that my competitors never understood.

I knew that most of our customers were women, 45 – 65 years old. The lady ordering our kind of products was more familiar with going to her local store and touching and feeling the fabric AND getting to see exactly what the colors looked like.

On the web you couldn't create that confidence. So we offered to send them a sample of the fabric from our bedspreads and comforter ensembles as well as our drapes, curtains and shower curtains.

The customer now knew the quality, thickness, and design of the fabric and had more confidence we were the kind of company she could trust. Building trust was the most important part of the equation that made our company the largest in our niche on the Web at significantly higher prices.

Then last, we added an amazing USP for our industry. "We'll ship it the next day for free, you can keep it for a full 90 days to make sure you like it, if not we'll pay to send it back and refund all your money no questions asked."

More trust!

This hit home with our customer and she loved the convenience. In a later chapter, I'll tell you a really big secret about this unprecedented 90 day guarantee. That is a fascinating story all on its own. Because we had created a more trusted internet catalog, with just what the customer wanted, she was willing to pay us more for our products than at other stores on the Web.

The truth is we did not have some weak, dull USP that no one really understood or cared about. We "knocked her socks off" with a USP designed specifically around what our customer wanted from an internet home-decor company like ours. We gave our prospects a USP none of our competitors were willing to match. That gave us a significant competitive edge.

A little side note here. We did find that some websites on the web offered a piece of our USP. We began to see a few 90 day money back guarantees for instance. But none were willing to institute our complete USP and probably wondered why it didn't make that much difference.

You need to discover what your customers want AND what you can deliver that will make a significant difference between you and your competitor. Create that plan and you are well on your way to creating a marketing system that will truly "Knock the Socks Off" your prospects and customers.

You will stand out in a boring world of "me too" businesses.

Chapter Five

Prosper No Matter What The Economy Is Doing

As I write this book, our country is in the throes of a deep recession. And it does not look like we are going to emerge from it any time soon. You will see some small up ticks in the economy, but mostly you can expect it to be anemic for at least 4-10 more years.

I highly recommend you study the information that the business economist, Howard S. Dent, publishes about what is happening with our economy.

He has had the best track record (that I can find) of predicting the general ups and downs of the economy over the last 25 years. He not only looks at long term economy trends, he wisely factors in the effect of population trends in the U.S. and around the world.

The state where I live, New Mexico, is a perfect example of why the economy is going to struggle for some time to come. It also reveals why many business owners struggle and sometimes fail. Okay, I get to have one little rant in this book. And here it is.

Why is it that several years ago when oil prices were booming and the state government was bubbling over with $400 Million in new tax revenue from oil and gas leases, state legislators and then Governor Richardson could find tons of places to spend that money like it would never go away?

B-u-t then a slowdown in the economy arrives and all that excess revenue evaporated. State income tax revenues were down because business and personal incomes were down. Gross receipts taxes were down because people were not spending as much.

However for some reason, Governor Richardson and our state legislature could not figure out what to do. They suddenly were short about the same $400 Million they gave away earlier.

Why couldn't they find all those new places they found to give money away and take it back again?

N-o-o-o, they are wringing their hands. They can now only find about half that loss in revenue to pull out of their spending. If they do more, starving children will die and school teachers will not get paid.

It suddenly seemed urgent. They just had to raise taxes on everyone to make up the difference. Recession is strapping businesses and people and we needed to help Santa Fe give more money away from our pockets without our approval!!!

I say throw the dummies out. Okay, I'm through. I feel better .... well for about an hour or two anyway.

Do Not Let External Circumstances
Put Limitations On You

All the stuff that is going on in the economy and in government will cause you to believe you do not have a chance to do anything.

You are stuck with whatever the economy is doing and you do not have any control.

But wait, YOU DO. Getting rid of your traditional marketing systems and implementing real "Knock Their Socks Off Marketing" will change the dynamics of how you get your customers and prospects to keep buying from you.

But, you must keep filling your education bucket with smart positive marketing systems that attract your prospects and customers to your business despite what the economy is doing.

One caveat here, this will not be easy. But have you ever known anything worthwhile that was easy? You must work harder, be more focused and work more hours than you have ever worked before.

A slow, difficult economy brings one bright, Albuquerque morning sunrise beam of hope into your world. If you take swift action and use smart nontraditional marketing and advertising you can dominate your competitors like no other time when the economy was thriving.

A tough economy is when true genius and smart marketing stands out more than any other time. Your competitors are doing the same things they have always done and it IS NOT WORKING!

The marketing they are using, the customer service they are delivering, the advertising they are **desperately** trying to get to work is not much more sophisticated than the cave man going out each morning to kill some unsuspecting saber tooth tiger so his family can eat that day. And he must go out and do it again and again e-v-e-r-y day.

Most business owners must slay the dragon every day in their business to scratch out enough customers to keep the doors open. You much change that dynamic in your business.

Smart Repeatable Marketing

You should have smart, repeatable marketing going out every month/week/day bringing in new income. You should not be recreating the advertising wheel every day.

I was recently at a conference where Ivanka Trump, the daughter of Donald Trump spoke. Do not discount this lady's business skills. She is a very smart marketer and developer of key business relationships.

She told us that her father, The Donald, believes this is a time for "Dynastic Business Success". What does he mean by that? When we have struggles in our economy, businesses that are inefficient, who have poor systems in place, who don't know how to innovate, fall out of the marketplace.

That creates room for those who HAVE created a strong business based on smart non-traditional "Knock Their Socks Off" marketing systems.

When those inefficient businesses get out of the way, smart businesses like ours gain an easier foothold and expand customer bases like no other time in history.

Since we haven't had a really challenging economy in over 25 years, we haven't had one of these opportunities come along in most of our business lifetimes.

Why is this important for you to understand? If you don't grab the bull by the horns, if you don't clean your business house of all inefficiencies, if you don't work harder in the next 12 months than you have ever worked in the last 5 years in your business, YOU WILL GET LEFT IN THE GREAT BUSINESS DUST BOWL of 2012 to 2018.

Am I talking about this to scare you to death? ...to act like the doom and gloom media??? Definitely not! I am more excited about the opportunity for our businesses than I have been in many years.

Stop Looking Through Rose Colored Glasses

BUT, you must look at this through the right prism; view the opportunity for what it is; and understand that it will not be easy. Just know that you WILL have to work harder than you have EVER worked before.

But if you do, the rewards will be Dynastic (to use Donald Trump's description).

The point of bringing up Howard S Dent, Jr. earlier is that he looks at more than just the ebb and flow of recession and boom periods.

We had recession-boom periods in our economy on average about every 7-8 years up until 1985. They came almost like clockwork. It was a necessary ebb and flow of a free economy. Starting in 1985 however, we experienced the longest period of expansion in our economy's history. The reason? .... **demographics**.

I constantly drill demographics of customers into my clients' heads. Dent added the study of demographics to his predictions and that has made his forecasting more reliable than anyone else in the country.

41

It Is All My Fault

I want you to know that I am very proud of the following statement. Are you ready?

I'm the reason for this 25 year period of the greatest expansion in history, W-e-l-l, not me personally, but my generation. It's the Baby Boom Generation that has been aging through our economy. This big "pig in the python" population bump moving through the United States age life cycles created the largest boom economy in history. Why? Because this generation was in its peak spending years, age 42-50 over the last 25 years.

We were spending and borrowing like there was no tomorrow. Well, I am sad to say, TOMMORROW finally came. The last of the baby boomer generation is leaving its peak spending years. AND, the next baby mini-boom coming behind us does not start reaching their peak spending years until 2020 – 2030.

Why is that important to understand? As spending by a large generation of people in the economy drops (like the baby boomer generation) and is not immediately replaced by a later generation's comparable spending, the economy MUST contract.

Two More Slow Economy Factors

There are two more economic factors contributing to this slowing economy. Throughout history there are (almost like clockwork) approximately 40 year economic lifecycles and 80 year economic lifecycles. This has repeated over and over since the early 1700s.

But, here is the BIG additional problem for us. Both a 40 year cycle and an 80 year cycle are ending right now. We are about to get a double whammy. Again this is not to scare you into giving up! I tell you this to scare you into getting to work like you have never worked before. Get busy and create like you have never created before. Go out and find great marketing systems you can clone like you have never done before.

Let's now look at the reality of what IS happening and WILL happen in this new slower economy. Most consumer categories are off only in single digits, a few in the 10-15% range. What this recession is doing is exposing the weakness in the business model for many businesses. You see this displayed when you find too many restaurants at the same big street intersection with the same exact dining experience most of the time.....a POOR dining experience.

I see too many businesses that were started by people who said to themselves, "I'm tired of working for someone else, so I'll start a business".

"Let's see...that seems like a business that'll make me some money. I'll get into that business." That model may work in boom times, but fails miserably during recession times. However, if you get busy and create a significantly better model right now you CAN still come out strong.

I was visiting with one of my clients who owns a carpet cleaning business. It was a franchise they had bought because they wanted their own business.

They chose this particular franchise because they were convinced the equipment the franchise sold was far superior to everything else in the market. Because of that belief, they felt the equipment technology would make them successful.

But the flaw in the plan.....the franchise didn't give them any real marketing support. What have we learned so far? Smart marketing will have to be at the heart of any successful business.

But, in this case there wasn't any real training on how to go out and get customers or how to keep customers....how to make more money off the existing customers....how to create continuity of income with existing customers....how to get prospects to raise their hand and say they were interested sometime in the future but not right now. There was nothing but the equipment and a name.

This new business owner was convinced. Because they had the best cleaning equipment in the industry, that would automatically cause customers to beat a path to their door. You know: the old "build a better mouse trap theory" that almost always fails. I explained to this business owner that I could take any middle of the road cleaning system out there in the market and create a bigger business than theirs all day long.

The reason??? When it comes to carpet cleaning, few people really understand the difference between one cleaning system and the next. The prospect expects every company to say theirs is the best system. The prospect knows intuitively, everybody isn't the best, but he doesn't have any real way to know the difference. Where can the prospect really tell the difference? They discover it in the expertise of the company and its owners, the quality of the customer service and the follow-up.

If I create a more effective system of informing the prospect and delivering these, I can beat the best equipment in the industry all day long.

You <u>CAN</u> Prosper In A Slow Economy With The Right Systems

That's why you must concentrate on the following "3 Prosper in a Recession Systems" to weather this recession storm and grow your business.

Having a great brand, the best equipment, the most experienced installers, even the best delivery system will no longer create success for your business.

In a slow economy you need more!

The Prosper In A Recession Marketing System

1. **Solve The Prospect's Perceived Problem or Need:** You have to recreate your business systems to solve a specific or group of specific problems your prospects believe they have, recognize and are willing to spend money to solve.

2. **Create a Commanding Customer Experience:** You have to create a customer experience that is so different from what they see everywhere else that they are drawn to you and become raving fans.

3. **Establish Authority Position:** And third, you must demonstrate to your prospect world that YOU are the authority figure in your business category. When you accomplish this, they will seek you out and only want to do business with you.

Sounds like a tall order doesn't it? I'm sorry....did I indicate this was going to be a walk in the park? This IS hard work, but the rewards are so great that it is well worth the effort.

First Roadblock to Small Business Marketing Success

But here is the first roadblock for everyone. You may be saying to yourself, "because the economy is slow and everyone has stopped buying, I have to cut back on expenses. As a result, I must personally do more of the delivery of my services or products to make ends meet. I'm covered up. I'm so busy working IN my business that I don't have time to work ON my business."

I understand that frustration. But this is a time when you don't have a choice. If you don't invest some time developing "Knock Their Socks Off Marketing" systems, you will suffer and your business could possibly die.

In a slow economy, more business and new customers will come far harder, than in the past. You will not be able to just have a business that depends on referrals for the next few years. You are going to have to actively market your business to attract more customers.

So that means you must give up something you enjoy doing...give up sleep...something...to give you more time to work ON your business.

In all economic times there are two groups of people in the economy. There are those with the "Willingness to Buy" and those with the "Ability to Buy".

The Ability To Buy

The "ability to buy" is one factor that you cannot effect. The lower 1/3 of the economy has been challenged with its **ability** to buy.

You cannot do much about that, unless you are a WalMart....who has a significant low price advantage.

But in all economies, in almost all business markets, there are still those who have the willingness to buy. Even today, with the economy struggling, with many losing jobs, cigarette smoking is still not dropping.

Most cigarettes in American are purchased by people who make less than $40,000 a year. The price of cigarettes is now $6 - $8 a pack. That's $120 a carton. But smokers are still finding the money to buy them.

The point here is that most people and most businesses have something in which they have a significant interest or significant need and where they are still willing to part with their money for products or services.

The Willingness To Buy

Frequently, I drive by the Harley Davidson dealer on Alameda Road here in Albuquerque. On the weekends, there are riders coming and going constantly all day long.

I never go by this dealer that I don't see a bunch of Harley riders pulling in and a massive number of bikes sitting in the parking area.

Many of these Harley owners have cut spending in other parts of their life but not on their passion – riding Harleys.

Selling leather riding clothes, Harley emblem products and accessories to Harley bike owners is one of the fastest growing industries right now.

Why in a tough economy like this is this industry expanding? It is because this crowd still has the WILLINGNESS to buy for a passion they possess. They may have cut back in other areas of their life, but this is a passion and they will sacrifice somewhere else to feed the passion.

You need to sit down and take time to analyze what niche groups in your industry have the "willingness" AND the "ability" to buy what you sell and deliver. Once you have done that, go analyze these niches and innovate in the "3 Prosper in a Recession System" areas.

I had a client that has owned an ornamental iron security doors and windows business for over 30 years. He has always done well just putting his name out there and getting his existing customers to buy more from him. But the economy had dealt him a severe blow. He told me that all of a sudden, people were not spending money on ornamental wrought iron. He was in a panic. What could he do to get the business back? I suggested that he needed to find a group of prospects that had the "Willingness" and the "Ability" to buy and "**Solve Their Perceived Problem or Need**".

What might that be in his business?

Well, with the economy slowing down, and higher number of people out of work, the home burglary rate is on the rise. If your home or the home next door was broken into and robbed, you suddenly develop the *"Willingness to Buy"* and many times you will do whatever it takes to have the *"Ability to Buy"*. I suggested he focus all of his marketing on this group of people. Find a way to know when someone's home has been burglarized and send commanding offers to them and all of their neighbors.

So your first order of business is to find a group of people who will have the "Willingness to buy".

Start Asking Questions

Once you have identified the niche group your next step is to answer some questions. What are some problems or pet peeves of this niche group that are unsolved by all or most of your competitors?

Do not try to answer this question yourself.

When I work with a new client one of the first questions I ask is: "What do your prospects really want from a company like yours, what gets their blood boiling, what's not being served?"

Almost always they give me the wrong answers. That's because the business owner is too close to the business.

I host several Platinum MasterMind groups of small business owners. When the group members are discussing why they belong, they all invariably talk about the one biggest benefit.

They will often say, "I can see what needs there are in other people's businesses but I cannot see it in my own business."

And that is almost always true. The reason? You are too close to your business. You are **too** caught-up with, preconceived notions like the carpet cleaner: "we have the best product in the market and that should be enough."

So how do you solve this problem? Actually it's really easy to do. You can do it with just 6 simple words. "Go ask your customers and prospects."

You would be surprised what customers will tell you. You may even be surprised what it is they want and will pay for?

Uncover the REAL Prospect Need

I worked for some time with the owner of a small CPA accounting firm. She offered her clients an option to work with them throughout the year to keep their taxes low for a simple, ongoing monthly fee.

Pretty much everyone declined her offer. When she introduced the idea to my MasterMind group, they gave her a whole list of things that would be valuable services she could provide for which they would be willing to pay more money. But, the list was not just about taxes. The prospect business owners wanted more from their CPA but WERE NOT getting it....Big Opportunity!

I recommended this CPA contact all her clients and give them a list of the services she could provide them during the year and the benefits to their business. Then she should ask her clients what more would they like to have from a business financial consultant, an on-call CFO rather than just a tax preparer. She was amazed at what they suggested.

She then could build this into her monthly cost, spread that cost over the year, and significantly decreasing their expenses over the year. She now has found a *"Willingness to Buy"* group. All because she decided to ask what they want, need and will pay to obtain.

Crafting the Customer Experience

The 2nd element, of our 3 Step "Prosper in a Recession System" is to find ways to **"Create a Commanding Customer Experience"**.

You have to make the customer experience so completely different from what any other business like yours delivers.

Let me give you an example. I am working on a marketing system for Auto Repair shops. I'm testing some of these ideas and systems in one of the auto repair companies here in Albuquerque.

The biggest untapped market for auto repair shops is women. Increasingly, more women have an automobile in their own personal name than ever before. More and more women are the ones taking a car in for service and repair.

However, just ask any group of women standing around in a room, what their experience has been going to an auto service or repair shop and stand back. These women will talk for an hour about what they hate about going to an auto repair shop. How they hate the experience and the feelings they have dealing with auto mechanics.

They will tell you horror story experiences of how they were treated AND many times flim-flammed into spending too much.

In fact, one lady told me she had paid $50 at one car repair shop to have the air flushed and refilled in her tires. I cannot believe the car shop owner could keep a straight face while making that recommendation.

But go into 99% of all repair shops and they are all failing at the things ladies want to experience. I bet there are a bunch of things people want from a business like yours that they are not getting.

Find them and go to work on them in your business.

All of these complaints are easy and cheap to fix. AND, when fixed in an auto repair shop, these changes bring a lot of word of mouth advertising. I guarantee the ladies will tell all their friends what they found.

But why do auto shop owners refuse to make changes? They are too busy repairing cars—working in the business rather than on the business.

Where is the parallel in your business? Are you concentrating on "Creating a Commanding Customer Experience"?

What Is Your Authority Position

Third and last of our "Prosper in a Recession System" is probably the most important of them all. All three are critical, but this one is the one most neglected: **Establish Your Authority Position**.

You need to find every way possible to demonstrate to your niche markets that you are the Expert. I know you have heard somewhere that an "Ex" is a has-been and a "spurt" is a drip under pressure and you don't want to be a "has-been drip under pressure".

Right off the bat, you must get that image out of your head!

Let me ask you a question. If you needed Lasik Eye Surgery in order to see, where would you go to seek help? If you had the choice between two eye surgeons that had Dr. in front of their name, how would you go about choosing the one that would be best for you?

Both have a specialty designation to work on eyes. But one has performed hundreds of successful Lasik surgeries, trained at the top Lasik surgery school in the country, written several articles and a book on the best methods for recovery from eye surgery and has appeared on television several times to let everyone know these facts about him or her.

Or would you rather have the surgeon that has all the latest scalpels, nicest gowns to wear in the surgery room and sends flowers to your room after the surgery?

You'd want the one that has demonstrated his or her qualifications in media and appears to have taken more steps to understand the problems associated with eyesight surgery.

You need to create the same in your business.

If you are the only one producing industry white papers and consumer guides, speaking before groups, creating free reports, audio recordings on CD, DVD presentations, teleseminars and webinars on your industry, you will set yourself apart from all the others.

Become an Author

Would you like to hear the best strategy of all? Sssh, don't tell anyone else. It's a secret. Write a book. I know, I know, you can't do it. That's why you must do it. After all, look at the word "Authority". Have you ever noticed that it starts with the word "Author"? That is not an accident.

Everyone else in your industry is saying the same thing. All of your customers think that if you write a book you are tops in your field. That is not necessarily true. But that is what people believe. They want to do business with the person that wrote the book on that.

A friend of mine, D.J. Heckes, owns a tradeshow booth construction and sales company here in Albuquerque, "Exhib-it Tradeshow Marketing Experts". She is very successful at growing her business in a very competitive field.

She holds free monthly business seminars at her offices. She has excellent speakers come in and deliver on a number of different subjects. She had a tough time getting more than 15-20 people to attend each month.

She started promoting the fact that she was finishing her book on "Social Media Marketing" to all her mailing list.

She told everyone in December it would be out and available at the seminar in January. At the January monthly seminar, she had over 40 people there. And, the seminars after this one grew larger and larger.

Much of that growth happened because she was now a published author. People now think she must know things others do not. She must have a greater level of knowledge that they could learn from her and her business.

Her prospects now believe she must know more speakers that have better content. None of these are necessarily true, OR, they are definitely true but without the book, prospects would not perceive her that way.

Who would you want to do business with, the person that wrote the book on auto repair service for women or the grubby shop down the street?

Remember, even during a recession there are still a lot of people with money to spend. You just need to identify who they are and give them the overwhelming reasons for spending it with you.

Chapter Six

Fishing With The Right Bait

As I work with clients to design evergreen marketing campaigns that return an ample Return on Investment (ROI), I often find the biggest mistake they make is **Fishing With The Wrong Bait.**

Now I'm not saying that all your customers and prospects are slimy little fish trying desperately not to get hooked every time you want to sell them something. However, many prospects do act like the Redfish I used to fish for around the Gulf Coast in Texas.

At certain times of the year, I would take my boat to the far back reaches of the Galveston Bay complex. There back in the shallow flats you would find Redfish feeding on the bottom.

I could actually see their tail fins sticking up in the water as they rooted for a tasty treat. So I knew exactly where they were. And, I knew exactly where to cast. Yet, if I cast my bait too close to them, they would spook and I'd watch that tail fin disappearing into the distance, no fish for dinner.

I soon learned, through trial and error, that I had to cast beyond where they were tailing and slowly bring it across their feeding path and let them discover it for themselves. Then, I would often get a strike and away we went with a wild fight.

There is nothing like hooking a big red fish in shallow water on light weight tackle for a real adrenaline rush.

However, if the bait I was using wasn't something similar to what they were eating on the bottom, the fish would just ignore it and go about its normal activities.

Your prospects do the same thing when you ask them to buy something.

I often discover this when I'm working with new clients. The client doesn't really understand their best market and consequently is casting the wrong bait. The prospect either ignores it or is spooked and quickly swims away.

Think of it yourself. At some time, you've been in a room full of people you don't know. Maybe it was at a networking event of some kind.

There are three or four of you standing in a group and an insurance agent walks up and introduces himself. And, insurance agents ALL make the same mistake of saying: "Hello, I'm Wayne Story with THE Blankety Blank Insurance Company."

What's your first reaction?? Run for the hills, right? Or, maybe you are a little more subtle than that.

You think quick and come up with someone in the room that you just <u>must</u> talk to at that moment and excuse yourself from the group and walk away.

You're not being rude; you just don't want to get caught talking to an insurance agent when you have insurance already and don't think you need more.

And, insurance agents are all taught they have to be persistent at requesting an appointment with you. So you definitely do not want him or her <u>persisting</u> on you.

Choose the Right Bait
From the Tackle Box

What is the problem? There are actually two problems with this particular situation and they are both sides of this issue of "Going Fishing with the Right Bait".

<u>First</u>, if you are the insurance agent wanting to get the best use of your time, you should have a definition in your head of who is a prime target prospect and who is not. This is a room full of a universe of random prospects. There is nothing in the room that inherently tells you which of these people is a good target prospect for your business.

<u>Second</u>, you should have a predefined message for your target prospect. The message of the insurance agent was so generic that it immediately sent the fish scurrying for the corners to hide.

Just as a beginning illustration of this "Fishing With The Right Bait" concept, I want to use a very familiar situation to help you paint a Technicolor Movie in your head that helps make this concept real to you.

Consider this room full of prospects at a networking event. Maybe it is an official Chamber of Commerce networking event, just for illustration. This is a room full of business people. And, let's say you own an auto repair shop.

You say to yourself....SELF....just about everyone in this room can use my auto repair service. They all have cars. They all need repairs on their car from time to time. So everyone is a hot prospect.

The truth is.....that IS NOT the case.

Our first problem, no defined prospect definition, raises its ugly head. And you can take this to the bank, **everyone in that room is NOT a good prospect**.

Some have cars that are new and still under dealer warranty and they bought a service policy that takes care of everything for the first 3 years.

Others may just love to go out and get grease under their fingernails and do their own car repair. So if you assume everyone is a prospect, you make a BIG mistake and limit your success rate.

The second problem you must solve is aggravated by limited time. There is no way you have enough time to meet and have a relevant conversation with everyone in the room.

You must ferret out only the people who are good prospects and engage them in a two way conversation that will move them into your warm, responsive prospect database. In this case since the group is random, you must quickly deal with both problems simultaneously.

You may be able to narrow the field by identifying potential prospects by age or some other demographic in your current customers that you know are prime prospects for your auto repair shop.

As you approach someone, you should ask a couple of questions to begin the conversation before you introduce yourself or your business. The purpose of the questions is to eliminate unlikely prospects so you do not waste your time.

Next, you need to deal with the second problem in order to increase the successful outcome of the time you invest in this type of prospecting. This is even more important now, in this new challenging economy, than ever before. You must get the most return for your time and money invested in each and every type of prospecting for new customers that you do.

Craft the Right Message

The second problem is having exactly the right message for the chosen best prospect definition that is most likely to bring you the most responses in a short period of time.

That is a lot of right, best and most isn't it?

The insurance agent's first message to this random group was: "Hi, I'm an Insurance agent and I'm here to bug you to death until you give me an appointment to come see you." W-e-l-l, that was not exactly what he said. But that was the message that came through the "salesman filter" in everyone's head, right? So in this situation, you should identify the type of prospect that is most likely to respond to what your business offers, and craft a message that will peak that targeted groups interest.

There are several methods to determine what crafted message (the bait) should be delivered, but I am only going to discuss one here. One method would be to ask a couple of questions that quickly defines for you if this person is a good target for your product or service and reveal their hot buttons.

Let's use the auto repair shop as an illustration. You have defined that a great target for you is a women who has had a bad experience getting their car repaired in the past. Instead of walking up and saying, "Hi, I'm Wayne Story, I own an auto repair shop over on San Mateo Blvd", you ask the following question. "Hello, I'm Wayne Story and I'm taking a survey of women and their auto service and repair experiences. May I ask you just three quick questions?"

1. First, how does taking your car into an auto service center or auto repair shop make you feel?
2. What kind of experience have you had with repair shops?
3. What should they have done to make the experience more satisfactory for you?

You'll immediately find out the ones who have had bad experiences. The prospects will quickly define themselves as someone who would welcome an opportunity to do business with an auto repair shop that solves her concerns. You have defined the right bait and allowed the fish to discover your bait. Now she will be ready to hear you out and allow you to put her on your prospect list. She might even respond to a special offer for a deeply discounted or free oil change right on the spot.

Do you see the value in this?

You will quickly find those who have a problem that needs solving and you will not waste time on people who don't have a need you can fill.

Wayne's Rule
Time Is Money – Especially When the Time Used Is Yours

What I've illustrated here gets at the heart of the problem when it comes to prospecting customers for most business owners. Not having a well defined message (bait) is the primary reason many business owners have convinced themselves that a particular advertising/prospecting method or media fails.

Almost all types of media WILL work for almost all businesses, IF we deal with this significant problem, "Right Bait for the Right Fish".

Missing a Defined Prospect Profile

Few of the client prospects that call me for consulting have ever developed a really good detailed profile of their best prospects. AND, their marketing/advertising systems grossly reflect it.

Most are too worried about missing someone who MIGHT respond to their message rather than those who are MOST LIKELY to respond to a targeted message. As a result, their message is big and broad and fuzzy and appeals to hardly anyone. Actually, I'm wrong. This approach can appeal to the prospect that has already decided they need your product, has decided they need it now, and does not know anyone who can give it to them. The big hairy problem is that there just ARE NOT enough of those prospects out there.

An immediate bell goes off in my head when I ask a client to describe who in the universe of people or businesses out there are most likely to buy their product or service.

Almost always, the conversation goes something like this. "Mr. Client, give me a profile of the best prospects for your business." Response: "Well, just about everyone can use my product (service). Anyone who has a car needs to have that car repaired at some time and that's what we do."

Here's the problem with that prospect profile. The bait you use must be very generic to talk to such a diverse audience as "everybody". It has to be so general that it doesn't hit anyone's pain or particular need. Result? Few respond.

The first action you must take is to complete a really good profile of your existing customers. Identify some commonalities among the folks you have sold in the past and determine what it is that motivated them to buy from you.

80/20 Rule of Business

Remember the 80/20 rule? It just seems to always work out this way. About 80% of your business will come from about 20% of your customers, OR in this case, 20% of a certain customer type or profile. You will also find that 80% of your problems, returns, complaints and time consumption will come from 20% of your customers.

Here is the rub. Far too many businesses I coach are spending 80% of their time, 80% of their marketing/advertising dollars, 80% of their inventory, 80% of their mental work capacity serving the 80% that only bring in 20% of the revenue. This generally happens because the business owner is too busy to invest time in really defining the best market, and selling only to that market definition. It's funny how many people spend hours creating a comprehensive "Business Plan" but almost no time creating a comprehensive "Prospect Definition and Marketing Plan" to go with it.

But YOU aren't going to do that, r-i-g-h-t??? You are going to initiate action to succinctly identify an in-depth profile of your customers.

You are going to identify the customers that are bringing in your best revenues. These will be the ones that are less likely to complain, are easier to sell and will bring you the greatest return on your investment?

Business Grows Faster When You Look For the Hungry Schools of Fish

Once you have a good profile of your best customers, it is far easier to find more just like them.

Why else is this important? I don't believe in "generic" persuasion. In fact, it is my contention that truly understanding the target prospect/customer is more important than any other element in the marketing process.

Yes, a "top of the heap" copywriting pro like Dan Kennedy can sometimes create offers, pitches, copy, etc. that will get satisfactory results even with a market he has little understanding of – but it IS NOT a very good situation for you to be in.

In fact, I attended a one-time only "Coaching and Consulting" workshop that Dan Kennedy put on himself. You can imagine how many thousands of dollars I invested in that workshop.

There were only 47 of us in the room and Dan spent 2 days teaching us all of his personal success strategies for developing consulting clients and creating the right kind of marketing campaigns for them.

During that session he made a big deal out of how much time he invested obtaining an intimate knowledge of the best prospects to approach for his client.

The reason he gave us for investing about 40% of his time on understanding the business' best customers has stuck with me.

He said "defining the client's best prospect universe had more impact on the return on investment of the marketing campaign than any other element even copywriting skills."

First Step Understand the Market

When I take on a project or work with a consulting client, I do my best to totally understand that market. I want to know how it thinks, what its values are, where they live and what's unique about their psychology when they live in that particular area of the country. I want to understand what is in their background that will cause them to respond the way I want. I want to understand what Dan calls "Psychographics". What are the biases in their life that cause them to react a certain way to offers. Understanding their age and the bias that brings to the table helps you write sales copy that resonates with your prospect and causes them to respond.

You really must have an intimate understanding of your prospects to have the greatest success with your marketing. Consider a potential target market that grew up in the free love, flower power generation of the 60's and 70's. Did that target market turn from that lifestyle or are they still being highly influenced by that lifestyle? What words and/or images will they most positively identify with?

Most of the time on my first appointment with a new consulting client, I can almost always stump them with the question: "What's a detailed description of the customer most likely to buy from you?" Again most often the response is "just about everyone can use our product".

Then I request they be more specific about the individuals. The client will often say words like, "people who want to do business with a first class company that really understands their needs." Or, they might respond "our best prospects are looking for a company that is more interested in giving them a quality product than getting them the cheapest price."

Well of course we would all like to find those kinds of prospects. I'm sure you would never say, "I want to find the cheapest prospects out there that only look at price and don't care whether the quality is all that good. They just need it and are looking for some place to get it." These statements about the company's prospects may be somewhat true. But this is a response that will cause a business to grovel in mediocrity forever or go out of business in the not too distant future.

Why does my first question stump them? Why does the right answer to this one question have such a massive impact on the success or failure of a business? To answer that, we must look at where this vague, undefined response comes from.

First, most people either start a business by finding a product or service to sell, or buy a business from someone else, or are roped into it by a partner that says, "we're going to make millions, just trust me." Have you heard that before? I have twice, and lost money both times.

Starting With Product or Service Is Wrong

Almost everyone starts with the product or service and THEN goes out to find people or businesses to sell.

When you do that, the only marketing method the typical business owner knows is to go out and start talking to everyone. And sure enough their suspicions are right just about everyone is interested in the product or uses the product or service in some way. The new business owner may have sold the product to a young single person, found someone in their mid-thirties, maybe he also sold it to a baby boomer and an elderly couple. SEE! Everyone can use it.

But if you were to actually keep statistics on every person the business owner approached about the product, you might find something like the following.

Out of 35 young singles only one responded and bought. Out of 110 mid-thirties prospects, only 2 people bought. Out of 72 baby boomer generation people, 12 people bought. Then, out of 13 elderly couples only 1 purchased the product. That would confirm most business owner's expectations about the breadth of the prospect universe for their product. Everyone will buy it.

However, when I look a little closer, I find the following revealing statistics. The business owner actually had the following Sales to Contact Ratio.

- 3% close on young singles
- 2% close of thirties age
- 17% close of baby boomers
- 8% of elderly couples.

So, the Million Dollar question (and the right answer really is worth a million or more dollars to you), in which group of people should you invest marketing dollars and selling time? In this example it is the Baby Boomer and elderly couples. Most small business owners would exclude elderly couples because they only made one sale. But, it's not the number of sales you should be counting but the Return on Investment. In this case that is the return on number of prospects contacted.

Real Life Application of Prospect Definition

I had a client I worked with for about 3 years. She and her husband bought a new offering from UFirst

Financial that you've probably heard people talk about.

You may have even been solicited by one of their representatives. It is a computer software system that helps you pay off a 30 year home mortgage and other debts in just a few years.

You would no longer owe the bank. You'd own your home free and clear in just a few short years.

The two of them loved and believed in the product so much in their own lives, they wanted to offer it to other people they met.

She and her husband started going to networking groups and doing presentations with anyone that would allow them to come out. They were having abysmal results. When they came to me for consulting, they had only one sale and were ready to give up.

They just didn't understand. They loved the product. They used it themselves and were already set to be totally out of debt including their two year old house in just 4 ½ years.

They asked me, "It works, why didn't other people see that?" The two of them felt like it was just too hard to sell to other people and were ready to quit.

I started asking some questions. Have you noticed in this book how I tend to do that? I let them tell me all about the key values of the product. Then I began to apply those values to the audience that was most likely to respond to their offer.

Profile Those Who Have Bought

I also asked them to give me a profile of the one person who HAD bought the program from them. I then wanted to know the profile of the other people they were approaching about the product.

Both she and her husband were in their late thirties, I think. (You never want to ask a lady her age, right?). 90% of the people they presented the program were couples their own age or younger. The one couple who had bought the program was in their late 50s.

Both she and her husband had made the assumption that because THEY fell in love with the program, everyone their age would immediately see the value and buy it too. WRONG ASSUMPTION!

Here is the second flaw in their sales system. Neither of them understood the motivation for the target market that would most likely buy. Ergo, they were using the wrong sales strategy.

The two of them were both in the money business. She was an accountant, he was a financial advisor. So of course everyone would make the decision (like they had) based on the tremendous financial advantages this brought to people's lives – especially young families, right?

They were trying to sell the service by talking about all the financial and money savings calculation reasons for using the product. After all, that's why they bought. But they had a bias that no one else had. And they missed this important nuance. The two of them would normally go through this long presentation about how the house would be paid off in just a few years.

They would explain in excruciating detail how much interest the loan would cost if you paid on it over the full 30 years. Then they would calculate for the prospect how much money the prospect could bank if they were able to stop making house payments after only 7 or 9 years. What could you do with all that money to raise your standard of living, etc.?

This reminds me of the story about the lady that goes into the store to buy an electric heater. The salesman comes up and begins to tell her all about the BTU output, the broadcast distance and projection of the heat, safety grill on the front that stays cool to the touch and the energy savings from being thermostatically controlled.

He is going on and on, trying to be a great salesman. Finally the little old lady weakly interrupts him and says, "Sonny, all I wanted to know is if it'll keep a little old lady warm on a cold winter night."

You see most prospects do not want to know the features; they just want to know what it will do for them.

After my initial consultation with the accountant and her husband, I immediately identified the market definition that would most likely be motivated to buy.

Find Your Market Definition From Your Existing Customers

The definition came from her one lone sale. It was the older baby boomer or recent elderly homeowner.

I am talking about people between 50 and 65 years old.

Here is the message I matched to this better defined customer profile. "How would you like to never have to worry again about the ugly nasty bank taking your home away from you in your later years just because something, out of your control, affected your income and caused you to miss house payments?"

When my client changed her focus of only talking to people in this new narrowly defined target market with a certain home value range (mid-range in Albuquerque), sales turned around.

Using this new message, sales immediately (within 2 weeks) improved. In that first two weeks they made 5 sales. That was after 9 months of trying with only one sale.

Then she started being booked-up with appointments weeks in advance with people who were looking forward to seeing her.

That is the value of succinctly understanding the right fish so you determine the right bait that will compel them to want to talk to you. You must have a vivid picture in your head and on paper of those people who are much more likely to respond to your offer.

Reduces Your Advertising Cost

There is another really BIG benefit to creating a Cracker Jack definition of your best potential customers. Your advertising cost will drop significantly or bring you significantly more sales with the same expenditure.

When you target a specific marketplace, two outcomes happen automatically.

1. Money is not wasted on advertising to people who are not likely to respond.
2. You can now talk in specific language the prospect will understand, identify with and more likely cause them to respond.

Otherwise, you wind up using words and context that are so general that hardly anyone will respond. Hardly anyone will feel you are talking to him or her. Each and every demographic, psychographic, regional, background group has a different language of emotions and facts that cause them to respond. Bill Glazer, author of the book, *Outrageous Marketing That Is*

Outrageously Successful, has some strong language for this:

"When everyone's your customer, No one's your customer."

This is very true. I have seen more people fail in business because of this one miscalculation. In my monthly newsletter, I told the story about going quail hunting with my dad when I was a boy. I was about 13 years old.

You know how it is when you are a 13 year old boy, you know everything. Nobody needs to tell you anything. My dad gave me some general gun handling training and safety procedures when hunting. We went out in the field and a group of birds would fly up. I'd raise the shotgun and shoot at the flock of birds and miss every time. My frustration boiled over. Evidently I didn't know as much as I thought I knew OR, maybe it was just a bad shotgun.

I asked my dad, "what's wrong?" He was downing a bird almost every covey that flew up. I was getting nothing. It was the same covey of quail. I was using the same kind of gun. I had the same kind of shells. I was just as motivated as he was to get a bird. But I wasn't hitting anything.

He told me something that totally changed my hunting luck and skills. And, it has stayed with me in business all these years later. When he shot into a covey of birds, he immediately identified only one bird to track with the barrel of his shotgun. It did not matter how big the group of birds were. It did not matter which way the birds flew. From his perspective it was as if there was only one bird that flew up. He aimed and fired at that bird and almost always brought it down.

Instead, I would get excited when the quail took flight. I would jump up with my shotgun and aim toward the big grouping of birds.

The covey flight was so dense that if I just shot into the group all those little pellets in the shell would just have to hit something and knock it down. But it didn't. I was targeting this big group rather than targeting one and following all the antics it was specifically making to avoid having us take him home for dinner.

Narrow Your Target And Put More Prospects In The Bag

You need to approach your marketing the same way. Narrowing your target to one finely targeted group or multiple finely targeted groups will multiply your success rate.

When you know your market and:

- can better define your prospective customer,
- have a detailed analysis of who they are,
- understand what it is that makes them alike,
- discover where they hang out that is the same, and
- know what psychological factors are in their life that is most important to them.

You can do two very cost effective actions in your business.

First, you can more easily find a detailed list of people who are very similar and thus more likely to respond. Or, you can find publications they are most likely to read. You can find places where they hang out and advertise there.

Second, you can identify how to talk to them in a voice almost as if you climbed inside their head and were repeating what they were thinking already.

You can present the right bait to get them to bite so you can reel them in. If you don't understand the language they use to speak to themselves, the things muttered under their breath, if you don't know the terms and phrases they understand and are important to them, you miss the mark and never get the sale.

In the case of the bookkeeper selling debt payoff software, the message important to the target market was the fear of the mean old bank taking their home away when they are close to retirement. You must learn to speak your prospect's language.

That reminds me of another story. There was this young girl who had to do a report for school on elderly people and what they think about living in the United States. She decides to interview her grandfather. The first question she asked: "What was the biggest historical event that happened during your childhood?" The grandfather responded: "I'd have to say the moon walk." The young girl looked disappointed and asked, "That dance was that important to you?"

You need to know the context of your prospect's life and what different words and terms mean to them. The words we use are perceived very differently by different groups of people. Moonwalk to a young girl was about a Michael Jackson dance with a silvery glove. To an older adult, it was about tremendous achievement in a short period of time against overwhelming odds.

What are you going to do in your business to make sure you are using the right words and "Fishing with the Right Bait"?

Chapter Seven

Mine the Gold
On Your Own
Claim

Most businesses have a tremendous number of missed opportunity in their existing customer base. That is what I call your own personal business gold mine. You should be investing in your own gold mine as well as prospecting for new gold in prospects who do not know you yet.

My wife, Linda and I use a local dry cleaning store about half way between our house and our offices. Linda stopped in one Monday to pick-up the cleaning we had left the week before. When the lady behind the counter handed over the cleaning, most of my shirts were missing.

So the clerk began to look through the racks for them. About that time 4 other customers walked in and Linda suggested that she could help the lady find the shirts by walking up and down the aisles of cleaning to see if she could more quickly identify them. Maybe they were put in the wrong place. That way the lady behind the counter could help the others who were patiently waiting.

Linda looked through all the racks but still could not find them. Then suddenly Linda spied them on a rack near the worktable. My shirts didn't yet have a cleaning bag over them. They were just hanging out.

The employee then said something astounding. "I don't know what to do. The owner sold this place to some new people from Thailand and they don't know what they're doing. The owner asked me if I'd stay on but I'm not sure if I can. The ticket for your shirts says there is supposed to be 8 shirts but there are only 7. They've got to find the other shirt so I left the shirts on the rack for them to find the missing one."

You are appalled, right? Surely employees know better than to say things like that to customers that help pay their salary.

It gets worse.

By this time, the clerk had begun helping someone else. The new customer was concerned that the staff had not put the right amount of starch in his jeans. He asked the clerk to feel the jeans and tell him how much starch was used. She felt it and said it was medium starch. He said that he had requested heavy starch and there it was written on the ticket attached to the bag.

The employee's reply? "I'm sorry that's what they did." She gave no empathy for the customer's frustration. There was no indication of desire to make it right. Nothing!

If she was not the employee from hell, she might have responded, "I'm sorry the mistake was made. Jane the owner would be very upset this happened to you. We will immediately wash them again and use the right amount of starch and you can pick them up this afternoon. And, because we made the mistake, here is a coupon for a free cleaning the next time you come in." Instead the customer walked out the door muttering that he would never ever be back again.

#1 Easiest Person to Sell

The number one easiest person to sell is someone in your existing customer base, someone who has bought from you before.

So why do small business owners spend so much time crafting advertising messages and ads to get more new customers and spend little if any time getting more business from existing customers? Why is there little or no time invested training staff and crafting the message they say to customers during normal customer relations exchanges?

If you want your business to grow, you must invest as much or more time on the existing customer message as you do on new customer acquisition.

It is 5 times more expensive to convince a new customer to buy than to interest an existing customer in buying more. So why do business owners invest so little time providing a better experience for existing customers?

What you and your employees say to a customer during a normal transaction becomes the gateway to a blossoming and ever expanding relationship, like hundreds of giant hot air balloons inflating on the field at the Albuquerque International Balloon Fiesta.

Each of your balloons of carefully selected phrases will create a burst of color in the mind of your customers and will project the value of your business to the customer.

If those words and phrases are not pre-selected....carefully crafted in advance.....you and your business will miss opportunity after opportunity to get additional business from your customers in the future.

If you were going to write a sales letter to your customers or prospects, what steps would you take?

You would invest at least a couple of days designing the message. If you had your ear to the crack in the door of any of my small business workshops, you would know you **MUST** invest almost half that time working on designing exactly the best magnetic headline possible.

This letter is going out to prospects or customers. You are investing money in sending it out. It will attract more prospects to your business.

You will want it to be as right as it can be the first time out. You will go back over it several times and have someone else read it to make doubly sure that it sounds right when they read it. You want to make sure it has just the right powerful phrases to get your primary points across.

Invest In Your Customer Experience

So, why do business owners fail to work on the words they use when he and his employees are face-to-face, toes-to-toes, nose-to-nose or ear to ear (on the telephone) with existing customers?

You may think you and your employees automatically know the right words to say. I will guarantee if you recorded yourself, you would find that you and your employees say it a different way...every time.

Well Scripted Sales Calls

For a time, I was part owner of a mobile advertising business that we named "Big Flippin Ad Trucks". We used that name because as the billboard truck drove down the street, the signs would flip and change to the next customer advertising message every 15 seconds.

When I first started working with the owner of the company, I created a carefully crafted presentation for him to use when he made sales calls.

I worked hard on it for days. I looked at all of the specific selling points that we had. He and I worked together to make a list of all the key objections that bubble to the surface during a selling appointment.

I also designed into the presentation elements of independent research justification as proof of customer value using the prospect's industry.

After assembling all this information, I carefully crafted the language he would use on those sales calls.

I worked on the order in which the information was to be presented. I designed specific stories that would be told to demonstrate value. I labored hours to construct the presentations with specific high response, emotion driven words and phrases.

What do you think my partner did? He refused to memorize or practice the presentation. He would go out and wing it in front of the customer.

Then he would come back and complain that the "presentation just didn't work". No one responded to it. He explained to me that "prospects only buy advertising based on how much it costs and his product was just too expensive for most customers."

He had developed that opinion because of two critical errors in his presentation and thinking.

First, because he was winging it on sales appointments, he was just selling another advertising media. All he was presenting were the features. There was NO emotional appeal and there was NO value build for the business buying the advertising.

Second, because he had not given them any real reason to choose his advertising media over other types of competing advertising media, the prospect automatically went to cost as the primary decision factor.

My partner was not using our carefully crafted message to get more sales. He missed telling the emotional stories of the value other customers had received from using this media. He was not building the value of investing in our type of advertising.

The prospect was already familiar with the other types of advertising media and had used them in the past. This media was new. We could not allow the prospect to decide the value in his business on his own.

Don't Leave It To Chance

Selling and marketing must not be left to chance, OR your brain coming up with exactly the right words on the fly. Otherwise, your customers will probably also decide that price is their only judge of value.

When your customers call with the same recurring questions, you should have a specifically crafted and memorized answer that is presented the same way every time by you and your staff.

Remember, every conversation you have with an existing customer is a selling opportunity. You SHOULD NOT leave that opportunity to chance.

Planning Ahead Will Stop the
Gold Rustlers on Your Claim

If you have failed to plan ahead with a well de-signed message, it will slip beneath the waves of your busy business life and you will lose an opportunity to solidify a business relationship and even worse, miss a chance to sell something else to your customer.

As an example, an insurance agent may have cus-tomers that call into the office to ask questions about their insurance. Those answers should be planned and rehearsed because every one of them represents a sell-ing opportunity.

When the insurance customer calls, it is almost always the same frequently heard questions. These questions should trigger the staff to ask a follow-up question to solicit additional business.

A call about the deductible on their auto insurance might be followed-up after the answer with a question like: "I notice we don't have your home insurance on file. What company are you using for that right now? If we could show you how to combine your home and au-to insurance and save as much as 18% a year, would you be interested in evaluating that?"

In almost all cases, if the insurance agent's em-ployee answering the phone follows up with anything, it usually goes something like this: "Hey, did you know that we do home insurance too? It'd be a much better idea to have all your insurance at the same company."

Which of those is more likely to get you more busi-ness if you are an insurance agency?

The Gold Is in Your Existing Customers

You MUST treat the existing people that buy from you as if they mean everything to your business, because THEY DO.

I know, I know, that sounds like it ought to be automatic for all business owners. But it isn't. You as the business owner may personally do a great job of this but what about your employees? What are they saying to your customers? Or what about the people that deliver what you sell your customers? Are they treating your customers like they mean everything?

If you have employees, you need to monitor what they say to customers from time to time. You should also create specific memorized scripts for what you want them to say.

Most business owners leave it to the employee to figure out what to say when a customer calls or walks in the door. That may be one of the worst decisions you can ever make in your business. Your employees will often say exactly the wrong thing when confronted with a customer issue because they have no training. The employees don't do it intentionally, it just happens in the heat of conversation. Every conversation you or an employee has with a customer should be treated as a selling opportunity.

There Is Gold in Every Customer Interaction

At our dry cleaners, the script I would have had them memorize and use would have turned this into a selling opportunity. My response would have had the employee sell the customer on the fact that the owner of this dry cleaner cares about their satisfaction.

Second, it would demonstrate that the business owner believes the customer should not be penalized because someone at the business made a mistake. It should cost the owner of the business something for a mistake.

Customers CAN actually at times be frustrating, believe that or not. I know none of YOU have customers LIKE THAT, but some businesses do. Sometimes customers fail to make it easy for you or your employees to treat them nicely. The least bit of a mistake and they go off like a Roman candle.

I am really bad about reacting that way to any business that wants my money. I react that way because I am so frequently treated badly that I have come to expect it. I get irritated, really fast, when I am inconvenienced and nobody seems to care.

You need to remember where most of your revenue and sales should be found in your business...existing customers...even when they are frustrating. Many times customers become upset because they are so poorly treated by other businesses that they come to expect that is how your business will treat them.

Most of you have a set way that YOU, as the business owner, personally handle customers when YOU are talking to them. What YOU say to them under different circumstances. I recommend that you record yourself talking to customers. There are certain phrases you use that make the customer feel comfortable and valued and sells the value of doing business with your company. Have someone transcribe what you record and then turn that material into scripts that you require your employees to memorize and use. That way all correspondence with your customers has the same message.

N-O-T one made up on the fly by your employee. That is definitely a recipe for disaster. Okay that is enough with my soapbox. The next mindset change is to reverse your "Gold Plan". What I mean by this is always thinking of your customers as gold bearing money machines.

Your existing customer philosophy should be: "How can I get them more, better, faster, easier, higher quality, and more desirable things that THEY want?" This births a "Reciprocity Plan" mindset that creates a wildfire of future business value in your customers. If you really think like that your profit will come, as long as you are conducting daily business properly. You just cannot have a "Reciprocity Plan" attitude for long without ending up with more value in your business or product or service.

Another one of my clients owns an insurance agency here in Albuquerque. She is constantly looking for ways to add value to her customers. One day she discovered that her insurance company would give her customers a free starter life insurance policy if they were insuring both their home and multiple automobiles with the company. She immediately started sending out letters to her existing customers who qualified for this program.

Now, most people are not interested in talking to an insurance salesperson about life insurance, right? I know I'm not. But in Jo's case, the customers were calling her. In fact, over 70 percent of the people she mailed the announcement call her office for an appointment to get their free life insurance.

Now then, here is the real kicker. Over half of the customers that respond to her letter actually buy more life insurance or other insurance services from her. The customers had not planned to buy any of this insurance before she contacted them about the free life policy.

She found a way to help her customers by providing them a free benefit and they responded by buying more insurance from her......"Reciprocity Plan" at work.

Chapter Eight

There's Gold In Them Thar Hills, Start Mining

L et's look at some key ways to accomplish getting more income from your existing customers. First and foremost, you need a list of your customers. If you do not already have a list, you need to develop a database list of your customers and prospects.

I so often see businesses that cannot put their hands on a list of their customers and what they have bought or typically buy from their business.

This is critical to the success of your business.

The two most important assets in your business is not your equipment, vehicles or the products you sell.

Those are the assets that make the green eyeshade accountants happy when they fill out your business balance sheet. But <u>do</u> <u>not</u> be fooled by the accountants. The most important two assets in your business are your customer list and your warm prospect list.

With those two lists, I can rebuild any company in a matter of weeks after almost any disaster.

If I lost all of the other "official" assets in the business.....building burns, flood destroys the inventory, the virus monster destroys the computers, I can rebuild the business overnight with these two assets. If I am looking to buy a business, the first assets I look at are the customer and prospect list. They are far more valuable than the hard assets.

If these two assets are missing, I will pass on considering an investment in the business. I don't care what the sales are. I don't care how great the products are.

Without a good customer and warm prospect list, I am going to struggle to grow the business quickly. So guard these two assets with your life. In this day and time of computers make sure that duplicate copies of your customer data and buying history files are stored off site.

His Customer List Was Out Of Reach

I was working with an Auto Repair Business here in Albuquerque. The owner had the employees dutifully entering the customer's name, address, telephone number and email address in the computer, FANTASTIC!

Except for one.....itsie, bitsie, small little detail. When I asked for a LIST of those customers, so we could send it to the printer and send out some direct mail, there was an awkward silence.

You see, the shop owner had purchased a customer tracking system from a software company specializing in the auto repair industry. It did everything. The system would track when a customer needed their next oil change or other maintenance and send an email or a postcard automatically. The system would tell him what a particular customer bought in the past. It would give reports on what prompted the customer to come in for service or repair.

It would even remind the business owner what service or repairs had been recommended and turned down by the customer on past service opportunities.

BUT, there was this one, really **B-I-G** flaw in the software company's system. The Auto Repair Shop owner could not pull out a database list of customers from the software.

The software was set up to automatically send an email reminder when it was time for an oil change. But...it would not give him a list of everyone that didn't respond to the reminder.

He could look at an individual record (on the screen) of someone who had not responded to the service reminder. But, (and it is an amazingly HUGE B-U-T) he was not able to get a list out to send an additional postcard reminder. He could not get a list of telephone numbers to send a voice broadcast reminder.

So what good was the system? Sure it did some automated marketing, but what happened when someone didn't open the email reminder?

He was stuck. It turned out, when we looked more closely, he found that less than 10% of his customers were responding to the email reminders and getting the needed service done.

And, he was fat, dumb and happy thinking the system was working. He just threw up his hands and decided there was nothing he could do. Solve this problem; get that number up to 30 or 40% and his business skyrockets in a hurry.

The first and most important method for getting more business from your existing customers and key prospects is regular communication.

Who Else Wants Customers Who Come Back Regularly And Buy More?

One of the biggest holes I often see in small business marketing is the poor use of the existing customer list to get more business.

The "Number 1" easiest prospect to sell is your existing customers who have bought from you in the past. They already know, like and trust you. Why aren't you selling more to them? In order to sell more to your customers, it is critical that you keep up a regular flow of communications to them. If a business does send things to their customers, most are just sending sales material. Come in for our 10% off sale. Come get our latest new gizmo. You need to do more than that. You need to keep up a friendly relationship, not just a "please buy from me" relationship.

How can you communicate regularly in a way that is automated and gives you more opportunity to be friends with your customers and define yourself as their primary choice for your kind of business?

Newsletters Are A Business Lifeline

The best and the one every business should be using is the publication of a monthly printed newsletter. Dollar for dollar, a monthly newsletter will give birth to more income for your company than almost any other media in your business.

Now, just a caution, this should not be your only system for getting additional or new business, but it should definitely be one of the first added to your list.

Here's why I strongly recommend newsletters and why I will invest a significant amount of time addressing this marketing system in your business. In one of my Small Business PowerCircle™ meetings I conduct monthly with business owners here in New Mexico, I asked how many were producing a monthly newsletter.

Less than 20% of the hands went up. Then I asked the follow-up question. "Of the ones who are sending out a monthly newsletter, how many are getting more business as a result of their newsletter?" Everyone's hand was still up.

So why isn't everyone doing it?

Every business owner who starts a newsletter tells me that within 3 months it is producing more new business that 75% of the other marketing methods they are using.

So again the question, why isn't everyone doing it?

Here is what I have found over the years trying to help business owners improve their business. There is the 80/20 rule. Only about 20% of the people actually implement the key strategies in their business that will bring them great results. This is especially true if the strategies are new to the owner, or if it takes some work or research to complete. Instead of looking for new more effective marketing methods, most business owners feel like they just need to do more of what they are already doing but do it even better and hope for better results.

Wayne's Rule
HOPE Is a Terrible Business Strategy

Only about 20% of business owners actually get outstanding results in their business. The problem is most people are trading time for money in their business. Any new sales they get require THEM to go out personally and drum up the new business. They spend all their time BEGGING the universe to do business with them rather than spend 20-30-40% of that time ATTRACTING business.

A newsletter is a business attractor.

There is one big mistake most people make when producing their first newsletter. The business owner tends to fashion it more like an advertisement than a newsletter. It becomes just another one of their sales brochures. Your customers will refuse to value it when it looks like a sales pitch. The customer will decide that you are not adding any value to their life and they will stop reading it.

Newsletters Develop YOU as An Authority

Also, sales brochure newsletters will not achieve our primary goal of developing you as an authority in your particular field. You will just look like another salesperson in a saturated sea of sales people and businesses.

I am often asked by insurance sales people, "Can't I just use the really nice newsletter produced by my insurance company." NO! (Is that definitive enough?) Corporate produced newsletters are more of what I am talking about. They are almost all just selling the insurance company. Your customer will not pay attention to it and will stop reading. It does nothing to create a relationship between the insurance agent and his or her customer. That fancy full color newsletter is destroying your ability to establish yourself as an authority in your market and in this industry.

A Newsletter Disaster

Several years ago when the contractor was finishing up the construction on our new building in Rio Rancho, I realized I had forgotten to make any plan for signs for the building or for our companies on the front of the offices.

I called one of my PowerCircle™ members, Al Padilla, who owns a sign store to help me design something. I also called the owner of a Sign-a-Rama shop here in town. I called him because he had called our office and left me a message that they could help us with signage for our new building. Evidently, he had driven by the building and noticed it was under construction.

I interviewed both business owners about what I should do.

Al had all kinds of suggestions and recommendations. He presented himself as a consultant on how best to do signage on the property based on the budget we could afford to spend.

When I talked to the owner of the local Sign-a-Rama franchise, he failed to provide any consulting advice. He just basically said "we can do this and we can do that and here's a quote on signs." In other words he had a laundry list of things he could do. "Here, choose one."

Instead, I chose Al. Later the Sign-a-Rama guy called back and asked if I was ready to make a decision. I give him props for follow-up.

I explained that I had decided to go with someone else. I also offered to explain to him why his approach to selling his services didn't work with me, even though his signs were cheaper than Al's signs.

He listened and gave me several excuses. I recommended that he attend our PowerCircle™ meetings to learn some great ways to market his business and get more customers. He came once and never came back.

A few months later, I received an email from his company. The subject was: "Sign-a-Rama Newsletter". Evidently we had talked about using a newsletter to get more business in the ONE meeting he attended.

The format was very unprofessional. The "To:" was addressed to approximately 100 different email addresses that I could see. Here is the word for word first couple of paragraphs and the rest of it was more of the same. You will see a couple of my comments in italics.

"Hello from Sign-A-Rama, your all around custom sign store! Welcome to our new monthly newsletter. First off, we would like to tell you a little bit about us and what we continue to provide for you. Our mission at Sign-A-Rama is to continuously be a force for positive direction in the signage industry. (*What in the heck does that mean?*) We continue to strengthen our brand through evaluating and adapting new technologies in our industry. As a result of the most extensive training program in the industry, Sign-A-Rama provides the most skilled and knowledgeable experts in the sign and graphics industry. We can help you develop a custom signage program that works for your business."

"This monthly newsletter will give you, the customer, an insider's view on all aspects of what we do, along with pertinent examples of our craft and inform you of our monthly specials by focusing on particular sign types." (*Aren't I now just brimming over with excitement to receive the next one?*)

Blunder of All Blunders

Blaa, Blaa, Blaa, Blaa, and much more of the same! Now then, on top of being just plain boring, self-serving and uninteresting, he made some kind of a computer blunder and it was sent to me and everyone else on the list over and over and over, 23 times in a row.

Then I started receiving emails from 4 or 5 different people who "replied to all" (I hate that). Each person said things like this: "Please take me off this list. You filled up my inbox with this email that was a waste of my time and it kept coming to me over and over again."

If he had made the newsletter email about him and gave pertinent educational information that demonstrated that he knew some things that would be of value to his customers and prospects, he might have been able to overcome this email blunder....sending it over and over again. He could have immediately sent another email apologizing for the blunder and saying that he found out why it had happened and fixed it so it would never happen again.

Maybe he could have even made fun of himself for making such a stupid mistake. People might have felt sorry for him since they now know something about him personally and let him off the hook.

Marketing Education
Prevents the Blunders

The second point you can learn here? You need to be on a continuing education path so you learn how to do things the right way and not make stupid, unrecoverable mistakes like this guy.

But this guy came one time to our PowerCircle™ group and decided that it would be a waste of his time. He felt he knew enough and could do all this on his own. If he had stayed in PowerCircle™, he would have learned things that would have prevented him from making such an unrecoverable mistake.

But the real lesson I wanted to get across here is the "real purpose of a newsletter". The purpose is to communicate on a personal level with your customer base, give them information that is interesting, and provide proof of your special expertise in your business with information that surprises them. That **IS** working your Gold Mine.

If you live in New Mexico and would like more information and a "Free Guest Pass" to the author's monthly Small Business Marketing PowerCircle™ meeting go to the website:

www.PowerCircleNM.com

Chapter Nine

Keep Drilling Deeper Into The Mine

The next action to building a substantial business is digging deeper into your existing customer base asset by communicating additional offers that are compelling to your customers.

These offers and sales pieces should be separate from your monthly newsletter. You may include an offer in your newsletter but it should be a minor part of what is contained in the newsletter. Otherwise, your customers will stop reading your newsletter.

A separate sales letter or special should regularly be sent to your customer base. There are several media you can use to accomplish this. You can use email or a hard copy sales letter. But, two critical elements that must be in every one of these communications is a compelling headline and compelling offer or it is just a waste of time.

The best media to use to communicate these offers to your customers is direct mail. Because they know you, and trust you, they will open your mail and respond.

Up-Sell Your Way to Riches

Another area to get more business out of your existing customers is the **"Up-sell"**.

Whenever you are in front of a customer closing the sale of a product or service, you should also offer some premium version option of whatever you are selling.

If the premium version seems significantly more valuable to the customer, we find about 20-30% of them will take the premium version. Some customers just routinely choose the premium offer because they always choose the best.

If you had not offered the premium version, you would have missed significant added profit.

Let's say you are in the investment business. You are selling a basic entry level retirement investment package to your client. Consider also offering that same investment package plus a monthly report on its comparison to the other possible investments, plus a one-on-one consulting call for a premium amount.

Cross-Sell

All customers are at their most likely stage of doing additional business with you at two times in the sales cycle.

The first happens just as they make the decision to buy your product. Immediately offer to provide them another product or service or more units of the same product at a better price. You should have a Cross-Selling option built into every product or service.

In my website catalog company, we had an offer on the checkout page suggesting if they ordered a total of $150 or more on their order, shipping was FREE. Most internet customers are looking for free shipping and this gave us a way to get the order amount up to a profitable level while giving them what they wanted.

The customers would usually go back and find something else to push their order over the $150 total. And, often after going back through the catalog they would find things they wanted that went significantly over the $150. When they came back they were already trained to order more than $150.

I also created a script for our staff to make that offer when they were handling phone orders. Over 50% of the time the customer went ahead and ordered more to get over the $150 minimum.

Just find some way to offer a buying customer more.

The second best time to get a customer to buy more happens just as you have successfully delivered the product or service and the customer is excited about the purchase (assuming there is a lag time between sale and delivery of the product or service).

You should always immediately offer them another product or service right after you deliver the original product or service. The longer the time moves away from the delivery date the harder it is to sell them more.

There are several ways you can accomplish this task.

Follow-up Survey

One is to follow-up with a phone call to survey their satisfaction with the delivery of the product or service. Your customers love to give you their opinion.

There is an old saying:

"Opinions are like noses, everyone has one."

And it holds true with your customers! On the phone call (or in person), open up a dialogue about other targeted products or services you want to sell.

You could also send them a satisfaction survey to fill out on line. Reward them with something if they fill it out. Then after they fill out the survey, have your website automatically send them to a page that offers them something additional they had not bought before.

Discovered Opportunities

If you sell products in the home like a home decorator, you could offer them something additional as you finish the installation of a window covering (for instance) that they bought originally.

Maybe you notice they did not do anything in the bathrooms. You might offer them a special window treatment item that works better in bathrooms at a discount. Since you are already out there you can save time and money. Because you can measure right then and there and save expensive gas money coming back out at a later date, they get this special deal.

Down-Selling

Another strategy in your "Getting More Income Out of Your Customer" bag of tricks, is **"Down-Selling."**

This is the concept of offering your customer something less.

Why would we ever want to do that? We have just crawled over broken glass to get an opportunity to sell something to a customer, why sell them less now?

I do not know how good you and your employees are, but believe it or not, and I know this is hard to believe, (tongue deeply embedded in my cheek) but I do not close or sell 100% of the people that I talk to. Can you believe that? When I don't close on the initial offer, I always have something less that gets a smaller yes. But the key here is that I get a YES. Because of the emotional nature of people, they often feel bad that they just turned you down. They know that causes bad emotions for you. Many times they will take the "Down-Sell" because they feel bad about not accepting your first offer. Offer them something that will at least keep them buying from you....again, the concept of "making a sale to get a customer."

This is an excellent strategy for first time prospects. Your primary objective is getting them in as a customer, no matter how small the sale. Then you have time to demonstrate your superior quality of service that allows you to come back later and sell them more. They are easier to sell after they have bought from you the first time.

A/B Option

When you make additional offers to existing customers or even the initial offer to a new prospect, I recommend you always have an **A/B Option offer**. This could also be used as an "Up-Sell" or premium offer.

Let's say you are a financial investment advisor. You are offering them some type of ongoing investment package that gives them a great return but has a certain amount of risk. That is the "A-offer".

Consider adding a "B-offer" that provides a similar investment package but with lower risk and lower return.

It is easier to get a yes when the decision is between two yes options than when the option is take this one package or not. A Yes or No option always has a lower closing ratio.

Clients that I can get to implement even just a couple of these system see exponential growth in their business. The business that thrives has multiple systems for getting more income from their existing customers.

Chapter Ten

The Power of
Sustained
Contact

Another area for improving the lifetime value of your customer is the use of **"Multi-Step Follow-up"**. Once a customer has purchased anything, there MUST BE a series of automatic contacts that happen. These contacts might take a variety of forms. Here is a list of some of what you can do:

1. **Direct Mail letter:** You might send them a thank you letter that includes a survey asking what they thought of your company and their buying experience and then asks for a testimonial.

2. Follow-up emails: This ought to be a series of automated emails.

At our website catalog company, we sent an email immediately after purchase that complimented them on their purchase and reminded the new customer of the reasons why they chose us. It also offered them a 12% discount if they bought another $100 or more within 7 days.

A couple of days later, we sent them an email with a story of what caused the owners (my wife and I) to start the business and the passion we had for the products and designs we sold.

Then we sent another email a week later that included a "Frequently Asked Questions" list. Of course we...generously...included the answers.

And, believe it or not, we offered them a special on one of our products that was a popular add-on item at our website.

We were starting the connecting process to develop them into a lifetime customer. We also had additional steps delivered by direct mail. We did not leave the process to chance.

Customers forget about you or even get confused about where they purchased the product. Many times we would have people call us to return product and after investigating find they were not our customer. They had bought it from another website and were confused about which online site they had used.

3. Follow-up phone call: If the sales are big enough and can justify the investment in time, a follow-up phone call should be made to the customer.

Ask them how they feel about their experience. Then ask several probing open-ended questions that determine if they have an interest in other products or services now or at a future date.

4. Post cards: I have a friend that is a residential real estate broker. He sends out post cards every month to all of his past customers.

Each post card has a different story showing how he had helped a customer. Or, it has a testimonial written by a customer; or a story about a unique way he was able to help a customer get what they wanted.

Every one of the postcards asks for a referral or for additional business.

5. Invite to a "customer only" event: This could be a seminar or workshop you would provide. What better time do you have of selling a customer more products or services than when they come to one of your events and as a subset of the event you offer them something else to buy from you.

Another alternative is to invite them to a free tele-conference/web-conference event where you interview someone that has information that would interest your customers.

6. Birthday cards, anniversary cards, Thanksgiving cards, first day of spring cards, 4th of July cards, you get the idea. Choose some unusual holiday when most people do not receive greeting cards.

I was working with a retail jewelry store client. The economy had slowed and business had dropped. The owner was looking for ways to get customers back in to buy jewelry.

I asked the question: "What events in life prompt your customers to come back and buy more jewelry."

His answer was Birthdays, Anniversaries, Valentine's Day and Christmas. I said, "Great, let's start sending offers to them on the first day of the month of their Anniversary and Birthday."

"But we don't have those dates," he explained. They had been in the Jewelry business for over 20 years and were not collecting this valuable customer information.

7. **Automated Voice Mail Messaging:** There is a system that I use and a number of my clients use that will call your customers and automatically leave a message on the customer's voice mail from you.

You record it, and then the system automatically calls your customers at a specific day and time. If a live voice answers it gives one message. If it goes to voice mail, it delivers the message you have recorded that (if designed right) sounds like you actually took your time to call and leave the message personally.

Wayne's Rule
In most businesses, more money is made in the "Multi-Step Follow-up Plan" than in the initial sale

---

I talked about Steve and his auto repair shop earlier. He decided to buy another repair shop. It was not exactly located in the most desirable place to create a growing business.

In the fourth month, after taking over the shop, revenue was 207% more than the best month the shop had in the 3 years before he bought it. The original owner asked if he could buy the business back. He did not realize it had that much potential. It didn't until Steve implemented his marketing systems.

One of the many strategies that Steve uses is the Voice Broadcast Service. Let's say he has some type of special offer that is mailed out to customers to bring them back into the shop and it has a deadline 3 weeks out. He sets up a voice messaging call to leave a message just a day or two before the deadline for the offer.

He finds that over 50% of his response happens after the Voice Broadcast.

What does that tell you about the value of a deadline and a reminder?

8. **Offer a free report:** This is a smart marketing device I use frequently with my clients. I spend a pot full of time on this strategy with my clients because it is one of the most powerful you will ever use.

We are muddily plodding through the age of information. Statistics show that over 70% of internet usage is caused by people looking for information. Your customers crave information.

Just about everyone has a secret fear that others know something hidden from them that could significantly reduce their costs, improve their decision making or keep them out of trouble.

So why not help them with that fear? Are your competitors doing it? Probably not! Would that give you a significant competitive advantage? Definitely!

A free report, composed the way I teach clients and PowerCircle™ members to do it, is usually very much a sales brochure disguised as a report. You are providing some knowledge your customer needs and wants. At the same time, you are demonstrating your industry expertise. And who should they buy from but the person with all the knowledge. Teaching the prospect to be a smart consumer is a really powerful small business strategy.

The free report needs to be stuffed to the gills with valuable insider information. But it also ought to point to you as the provider of the solution to the problem **that information** reveals and solves.

As you create your free report, you must focus like a laser beam in a microprocessor factory. Focus on what the customer feels will be valuable information.

When I say it is a sales brochure, I don't mean that in the traditional sense of the term. I mean that it should be formatted with my **"FIP Formula"**:

- **F**ocus on a problem or group of problems that your customers face in your industry.
- **I**rritate the problem and give an overview of the solutions.
- **P**osition you as their primary source for solving the problem because you seem to understand it better than anyone else in the industry and are the only one telling them the "dirty little secrets".

Your existing customers are the biggest gold mine you have in your business. Do not let the gold vein play out. Keep digging for more and more profit.

Get My "Key Elements of a Successful Free Report" Small Business Guide

If you would like a list of some of the Key Design Elements that I include in the free reports I design for my clients then enter the following into the URL address line of your favorite browser:

www.KnockTheirSocksOffBook.com/report
Join my bi-weekly "Small Business Marketing Prescription Newsletter" and I will send your "Key Elements of a Successful Free Report" guide along with your first newsletter.

Chapter Eleven

Seductive Marketing Sells Faster

I know, I know, the headline for this chapter sounds like I'm going to discuss selling sex in marketing. I am not, even though there are a lot of advertisers on TV, Newspaper, Radio and email every day using sex to sell their products.

I definitely get enough of those type ads in my email inbox. Evidently, I have a significant malfunction in the sex department – because I am constantly getting emails indicating that I am lacking in that department and need their special pills or some personal device so that I can last longer in bed. But I digress.

That IS NOT what I am referencing here when I use the phrase and strategy I call "Seductive Marketing".

Hard Sell Is Out

America is living in an advertising saturated world and has grown very tired and suspect of the hard sell. Over the last 10 years or so, direct salespeople throughout the U.S. are finding it significantly more difficult to succeed with pressure selling tactics.

Prospects are zoning out as soon as they hear any kind of pressure sales technique or get a hint that the salesperson is insisting that they must buy now.

You may have had the sales training that goes something like this: "47 Ways To Close the Sale". After all, we know that if they do not take action now they are never likely to get around to it, right?

In today's world that is very WRONG, unless you are selling something that people DO NOT NEED. If you accept this in advance, you need a superior system to do well.

You need to construct an environment that seduces your customer into doing business with you, use your service, buy your product and trust you to give them a prescription for their need rather than a forced sale.

Your prospects would rather be reminded about your business and given reasons to respond that are more valuable to them (the prospect). Prospects in the 21st Century refuse to feel SOLD into doing business with you. In fact many are disappearing like ghosts in the night the instant they perceive this type pressure selling process. They immediately turn you off.

Seductive Marketing Attracts Customers

The concept of "Seductive Marketing" is really about setting up the sale so your customer is drawn to your company and seduced into doing business with you. The act of "Sales Seduction" moves you into the position of being the prospect's only smart choice to buy your products or services.

The prospect feels like they discovered you, not pursued by you and badgered into buying. The prospect should sense you understand their needs better than others and they will value the benefits your products or services bring to their lives.

Your biggest advantage with this type selling is that price becomes a minor factor in your prospect's decision process.

I use the following illustration in my free monthly "Small Business Customer Vortex Workshop™" and it is very appropriate in this discussion.

Speed Dating Decision Making

Most of your customers use what I call the Speed Dating form of decision making when choosing a company to fill a particular need. You know what I am talking about. There are these events held in cities all over the country where a lady goes into a restaurant or a meeting room and sits down at a table.

Then an endless stream of ugly and recently divorced, confused guys sit down to tell her their life story...put their best foot forward (if there is one).

She has a 5 minute discussion with each of these guys and then at the end of the evening has to a make major life dating decision. And, since she doesn't have enough information, she just decides to choose the least offensive of the bunch.

That is pretty well what is going on out there as your prospects choose a company for their product and service purchases.

It is exactly what happens for most people in the real estate business, insurance business, doctors, dentists, financial planners, pest control companies, personal coaches, event planners, interior decorators, and many more.

The prospect may not interview you or your company personally but they do it in other ways.

Prospects Flip Through Business Ads

The prospect speed dates the yellow pages or your website along with everyone else and makes a quick decision based on poorly understood and erroneous information.

I do not believe in participating in that process.

After she's through reviewing all the losers, I want her to call me because she's heard from one of her girl friends or something she's read about me that convinces her I'm one of the nicest guy in town and the best lover she would ever want.

And, she has heard that I know more about how to serve her real needs. I must find a way to help her understand that I know what it means to be a gentleman before she calls. You must do the same in business.

Let me prove it to you by bringing this speed dating idea home to the everyday business you and I have to conduct.

You know how it is; your customer makes appointments with several people in your industry, dances them through the office or home and then chooses one based usually on something that has nothing to do with the best decision making process.

Speed Dating Real Estate Agents

A perfect example of this is the residential real estate business. This problem is at the heart of why there are so many real estate agents and so few of them actually make a good living at it.

Here is a typical situation. This is not all the time, but a majority of the time it goes something like this.

A couple decides to sell their house. The homeowners have heard from some friends that it is a real hassle to sell your house yourself, so they should use a Real Estate Agent.

However, they don't know any Real Estate Agents they would trust. The wife opens the newspaper, or the yellow pages, or she drives around the neighborhood and looks for real estate signs.

She picks four or five real estate agents, calls them up and makes an appointment with each of them over the next week so they can decide who to use.

Sometimes, the real estate agents even allow the prospect to do this by phone.....WRONG!

All five of the agents come to the house, do their "Listing Presentation", and then the prospect picks one to be their agent.

Boring Cookie Cutter Presentations

Now in most cases, all of the listing presentations are about the same. The real estate agents are all taught the same boring script. So the homeowner really doesn't have any reason to pick one over the other. The homeowner winds up deciding on things that have nothing to do with selling their home.

If asked how they made the decision, they might say something like one of the following:

- "I trusted her a little more."

- "I like what he had in his presentation binder a little more."
- "He knows my brother-in-law's second cousin twice removed."
- "She's from my home state of Texas and I trust people from Texas more, etc."

The homeowners make an emotional decision that is not based on anything that will really benefit them. What SHOULD the homeowners be using to decide? How about things like:

✓ How many houses has the agent sold in this price range in the last year?
✓ On average, how many days do the agent's listings stay on the market?
✓ How close to the original listing price is the agent able to get for the house on average?
✓ What additional actions does the agent take besides list it on the MLS and do one open house?
✓ What knowledge and advice does the agent bring to the table on staging the home for best viewing and highest price?

These are some of the factors and statistics that ought to determine who the homeowners choose. BUT, seldom ever are any of these in the homeowner's list.

In fact, think of the last home you sold. Did you weigh any of these factors when deciding who to choose for your listing agent? I will bet hardly any of you did. In fact, I will bet that you did not even know you should consider these factors. Because as a business owner, you know so many people, you probably chose an agent you know or were recommended by a friend.

It is not because you are dumb and don't know what you are doing. It is because none of the agents you interviewed ever taught you what you ought to be considering and what judgment you should make.

They failed to "seduce" you into doing business with them by giving you the right information.

Stop Participating

I and my clients refuse to participate in this whole speed dating process. I want to set up the sale so that I am viewed as the prime solution or the prime value before I ever get down to selling face to face. I want to seduce them into doing business with us.

Hardly any lady wants her date to spend the whole night hard selling her on the wonderful reasons why she should feel privileged to get an opportunity to date him.

She wants to be wooed with actions and little discoveries of how he treats women with respect. She wants to discover that he has many actions and opinions that appeal to her. She wants to know that other women think highly of him. She wants to discover, through the little gestures, that he is her kind of guy.

She wants to be seduced NOT SOLD!

Prospects Want To Be
Seduced Instead Of Sold

This is what your prospect wants and responds to more and more in today's world.

I own a marketing consulting company where I coach business owners how to grow their business with non-traditional marketing and business design. I could do what everyone else does. I COULD just go out and cold call all the target businesses in New Mexico. I could:

- make a big presentation,
- tell them all the great things I've done and skills I have,
- and give them a laundry list of the types of services I provide.

But instead, I decided to take a more seductive approach. In most cases, I want the first real awareness of my skills and qualities to come as a result of attending our PowerCircle™ meetings.

PowerCircle™ is a monthly meeting of 60 - 80 small business owners who are learning and sharing non-traditional marketing strategies specifically designed for small business.

As the host of the PowerCircle™ group, I demonstrate skills and true value:

- with presentations,
- the people who get to present to the room,
- the testimonials others give,
- the personal stories of successful business owners who have used the training and consulting I provide.

Not everyone is at the state where they are ready... right now...to contract for a marketing strategy plan and/or advertising campaign designed by my company. So we help them move through the different levels of interaction with me and my company as they identify...and want to solve needs.

You should find a way in your business to move prospects along a pre-designed path. Your business will grow significantly stronger and create a long sustainable income when you have a "Prospect Seduction Ladder."

Chapter Twelve

Prospect Seduction Ladder

The key to all marketing systems is getting enough interested, warm prospects in your "**Starter List**" to create growth and allow the process to mature and improve the prospect's responsiveness. Once that is accomplished, you will have a dump truck load of customers wanting to buy your products or services.

Your "**Starter List**" is the group of names, addresses, telephone numbers and email addresses of prospects who have somehow indicated at least an interest in your company and what you sell. You may have often heard this called the warm prospect list.

From time to time I get referred to a business for marketing consulting. Sometimes the Chamber of Commerce or another organization recommends me and other times it is one of my clients.

But here is the problem. This new prospect has no history with me other than the referral. Immediately their guard is up and the business owner will almost always plan to interview several marketing consulting companies and ad agencies.

I Refuse to Participate

That puts me back in the speed-dating mode again. Remember what I said about the speed dating decision process? I refuse to participate.

For instance, one of the Senior VPs at the Greater Albuquerque Chamber of Commerce was working with a business owner that was new to town. He had purchased an old hotel in downtown Albuquerque. They were refurbishing it and bringing it back to its original glory.

The hotel owner needed some help with marketing in New Mexico because he had no previous experience here. It turned out their issues were much larger than that but that's what motivated the call. I scheduled the appointment for about two weeks out.

I had other appointment times available sooner, but I did not want to appear too hungry. Prospects will not respect your time or your skills if you appear hungry.

After booking the appointment, I immediately sent the prospect a box of proof items about me and my business (my "Knock Their Socks Off" package).

It included:

- A booklet I had written on key business marketing mistakes,

- Several CDs of speeches I had given,
- CD of a Teleseminar on a key marketing subject I had recorded,
- Several other Free Business Guides I had written.
- A booklet of information about the types of work we do for clients and the approach to marketing we take with clients.
- A whole booklet of testimonials and client stories, and
- A checklist of the key questions he should ask any Marketing Consultant or Ad Agency he considered paying for marketing services – most of which could only be answered by me.

My "Knock Their Socks Off Package" now includes this book you are reading. Most consultants might have sent him a three-fold brochure on their company at most, if anything at all.

If I was going to invest my time with him, I wanted to make sure I stood out as the "Andre the Giant" of Marketing over everyone else in the crowd. I wanted to lay a foundation for the Seduction Process.

Then about 3-4 days before the appointment, I called to confirm and asked if he had a chance to review the information I sent him.

He had not. My "Knock Their Socks Off" box was still sitting on his desk. I suggested that we delay the appointment until he had a chance to at least listen to one of the CDs and look at the client stories and comments.

This move is REALLY risky isn't it? I could offend him. I could put him off and he could decide not to consider me at all. But, my time is valuable. I don't have time to run out and do "listing appointments" all day and hope I get some business from it.

I explained that having him review the information was critical to getting the greatest value out of the time we would invest together because I am not like the average marketing consultant in Albuquerque.

If he did not have the information in advance to know what to ask of me and what to expect, we would lose valuable time that I know he didn't take lightly in his business.

I needed for him to take the time to review the information that would set me apart from my competition, "Seduction Marketing". I also wanted to make sure that when I arrived he already had a higher opinion of me and my company than my competitors. I was making sure he would be more open to our conversation and already predisposed to do business with me.

Stand Out In a Sea of Competition

I was also delaying the appointment to make sure I gave him time to interview the rest of my competition with MY checklist. I was creating a first appointment setting where I was in a position of strength as a prescriber of solutions instead of a salesman.

Are you beginning to see how this Seductive Marketing approach puts you in a better position to compete with others, have customers who ask your advice, and create less price resistance?

The prospect must know a lot about you, your business and how to make informed decisions in your industry before you are ever in front of them.

Now that I have defined the value and the Mt. Everest advantage you can create over everyone else in the marketplace, let's invest some time in how you might create a "**Seductive Marketing System**".

I'm going to cover the use of both physical direct marketing and websites in this process. I will address this primarily from the standpoint of a cold prospect. However, this also applies to a great extent when trying to sell additional products or services to current and past customers.

10 Step Prospect Seduction Ladder
Step #1: Luke-Warm Who

This is the ladder rung business owners foul up most often. It is the step of identifying the niche market in the cold prospect universe that is most likely to buy your product or service.

Where will you find the ripest fruit? This is the most important cold prospecting function of your marketing. In this step, you identify a small niche of the universe that you can easily find. As I said earlier in this book, you need to narrow down the prospect universe and choose a specific definition of the most likely prospects who will buy from you the easiest.

You must invest a significant amount of your time on this step. All of the rest of this "Prospect Seduction Ladder" will fail if this step is done poorly.

This definitely applies to the advertising process. You see, most people think that business growth is had with just the perfect TV or Radio spot or the perfect Yellow Pages advertisement. But the truth is this is only the first step in our "Prospect Seduction Ladder". Once you have chosen your target niche, you need to concentrate on doing something that gets your ad, direct mail piece or website read.

In the case of a direct mail piece, you should create something interesting in the packaging, or in the way the device is delivered that causes the "Luke-Warm

Who" to start reading the first headline and then the first paragraph.

Step #2: Interest Hook

Once the niche is identified, you will create an ad specifically targeted to the identified "Luke-Warm Who". This is where you start to design your yellow pages ad, direct mail piece, or display ad in a trade magazine or wherever.

For your website, it might be a Google Adwords campaign with just the right targeted and tested headlines.

You might also use a mailed postcard to direct them to a website where you do your selling and start the next step in your "Seduction" process. It is extremely difficult to get prospects to respond to a postcard and buy something. You have a far better likelyhood of selling something if you get them to a website where you have plenty of space to sell.

Step #3: Identify the Ripening Fruit

Offer something in the marketing piece or website that gets them to do what I call "raising their hand". Offer them something free or very low priced to make the threshold low for them to indicate an interest in what you sell.At this point, you are probably asking yourself, "why not just jump straight to the sale?" This is easiest to answer by illustrating it with a website example.

People constantly tell me they have a website that has thousands of visitors but no one buys anything. I had this conversation once with an author of two books she was selling on line. Even though she had the notoriety of being a contributing author to several "Chicken Soup for the Soul" books, thousands of visitors were coming to the website but hardly anyone was buying from the site.

In her case there were also other issues. But, there is at least one other step she should have implemented in her websites and in other media advertising. That step is to find out the names and addresses, or names and email addresses of as many people as she could who see her advertising or visit her website and have an interest in her message.

In your business marketing, you need some type of free or low threshold offer that causes your prospect to want to identify who they are and give you their contact information.

Step #4: Prime-the-Pump

When I was a kid, we had friends that lived out in the country and raised horses. They had a well with one of those old hand pumps to get the water out of the well.

You've seen them in old cowboy movies. It is a hot day; a couple of cowboys come in from the range. One sticks his head under this iron spigot, while the other cowboy pumps the big handle and the water flows out.

The problem was that if the pump had not been used in a while, the pump had to be primed. You had to pour some water into the pump to get it to interact with the water coming out of the bottom of the well and deliver more water.

Create Interaction

In most cases, you need to "Prime the Pump" with your prospects and gain some interaction with them prior to attempting to close the sale. Most business owners want to immediately proceed to selling the product. But there are far more prospects out there that are beginning to be interested but not yet ready to buy than there are ready to go buyers.

In this 21st Century, prospects are weary of companies that immediately start selling. Few of the prospects immediately go buy something the minute they have the first desire or need. There is a process they go through to get ready to buy. Inserting yourself in that process as early as possible builds the strongest business.

Send the prospect some free information. Create a follow-up of emails, or direct mail pieces, or free recorded messages, or voice broadcast messages, or all of the above that start a dialogue with the prospect about your products or services. You might offer teleseminars, additional free reports, webinars, access to videos, etc.

Get them to tell you with their participation in this process that they have a greater level of interest. Now you are starting to narrow the huge prospect field to the ones who will have a serious interest.

You do not want to waste scarce marketing dollars on people who only have a passing interest and are not likely to ever buy.

Step #5: Light the Fire

You have now warmed-up the prospect. It is time to begin kindling a fire for you and your product or service. You should start the process by sending them information about you, your company, testimonials, and case studies from similar customers. Tell them stories that explain why you are in this business. If it is needed, get the agreement from your prospect to send YOUR "Knock Their Socks Off" package.

Step #6: Make a Compelling Offer

It is now time to send your proposal or a special offer for your product or service specifically targeted to this prospect niche. If you do not include a specific offer, you leave control of the sale in the hands of the prospect.

Being weak in this step is why so many local bricks & mortar businesses struggle and fail during tough economic times. They leave it up to the prospect to decide to take action and buy from the business. Most businesses do not give the prospect a compelling reason to buy now.

Because the buyers are far more skeptical in this new economy, they procrastinate and do nothing.

In this "Make a Compelling Offer" step, your primary job is getting them to make their first purchase of your products or services. You want to make choosing to do business with you very enticing and easy.

You should invest some of your advertising capital building value by offering free bonuses, special services for free, etc. to go along with the offer. This step gets them to make the first real advancement from prospect to customer.

Awhile back, I was looking for a roofer to stop a leak in a rent house my real estate investment company owns. The person I normally rely on for this work was out of pocket. I went to the internet in search of another "Albuquerque Roofer". I found a video from a local roofer as the second listing on Google.

I called and explained my problem and he made an offer to go out and find the leak and patch it for just $300 - $400. He explained that most roofers want to immediately replace whole roofs but his company was skilled at maintaining a roof for its full life.

I am an investor. Knowing that most investors do not want to hear – "replace the whole roof" from a roofer, he made a small offer to get me to make a decision and let him come out. He was beginning the seduction process.

Once he arrived at the rent house, he found a number of spots that needed work. He fixed the immediate problem for the quoted amount. Next, he gave me a proposal for repairing the other problems that needed action to help the existing roof last longer and explained several secrets for getting a rent house roof to have longer life.

He now has my real estate investment company as a customer for all of our roofing problems. But it started with a smaller offer. He did not go for the whole ball of wax up front.

The result? He got my business. He understood my issues and crafted an offer that would get me to take action, now.

Step #7: Raving Fan

Your prospect has now moved to customer and taken the first step, exchanging THEIR money for one of YOUR products or services. Now, it is time to get a system in motion that demonstrates you deliver far above their expectations of anyone else in your industry.

If you want to keep these customers for life and have them refer their friends, you must create a "**WOW Experience**" for them. That means creating scripts for your staff to use when delivering the product or service. You and your staff should be using specific, pre-planned (scripted) language that demonstrates to the customer the long term value you will create for them.

For a time, I worked with a Periodontist (a gum disease dentist) to help him rebuild his practice. One of the first things I found missing was his patient experience and follow-up process. There wasn't one. The doctor's office was missing a follow-up system that reminded the patient of the value he had provided during their treatments.

There was no planning put into the handling of the patient after the procedure, the thank you note for using his practice, or the praise of the patient for taking action to improve their dental health, etc.

You must make that first experience light years ahead of anything they get from anyone else in your industry. You MUST NOT just sell and move on. This is what I call the "Customer Experience". What do they remember about the experience of doing business with you? What kind of follow-up comes after the sale? Or do you just get your money and run?

If the value is large enough you might even give the new customer an unexpected free gift. In our website catalog company, we always included a small gift in each box we sent out to customers. It was something they did not expect and said we valued them as a customer. The customer would often call the office just to thank us for the unexpected gift.

If you do not put in place an unexpected experience, you may create a sale, but you do not create a customer. Dan Kennedy once told me that "the primary purpose of a sale is to acquire a customer, not get a customer to make a sale." The only true sustainable asset in a small business is a "Raving Fan" customer list.

Step #8: Create Customers for Life

You have just converted a prospect to a customer...now what?

Start offering them other products and services that would be valuable to the customer and improve their life, or business. Start by sending a customer newsletter. Find ways to get their names in your newsletter. Get their testimonial and publish it in your newsletter. You will be surprised how much impact it has on customers to see their name in print.

If you have a doctor's office, an auto repair shop, a hardware store or some other type business where people walk into the business, make sure you put up their testimonials and photos on the wall to let them know you remember.

A Five Guys Hamburgers restaurant recently moved into our neighborhood. On their walls are big posters you can read from across the room. Each poster is printed with an award they have won or a testimonial from a media source like a newspaper or magazine about how fantastic their hamburgers are. That was very smart. Five Guys is reminding you that you made the right decision. Most fast food restaurants put up pretty pictures and special wall paper that does nothing to connect the customer to their business.

In this step, you are building a stronger relationship with your customer making it difficult, if not impossible, for your competitor to break that relationship. You want to be perceived as their reliable business partner.

Step #9: Trusted Advisor

After implementing the above steps, you are now poised to partner with your client or customer and be their definitive and only provider of the products or services you offer.

Let's say you are an insurance agent. You have convinced a particular business owner to get their car insurance from you. Then you show them how much you can help by providing home insurance, then maybe boat or motorcycle insurance. During these steps you have taught them how to make the right kind of insurance decisions. You have educated them about insurance issues they never knew. You may have even taught them how to save money.

They now see you as a primary provider of those basic services and are starting to recommend their friends to you.

In this step you create a system that causes the new customer to perceive you as their insurance and life protection consultant. They will only call YOU, when they have any kind of insurance question or need.

Anything...like business insurance, insurance on their building, pet insurance, life insurance, key man insurance, business liability insurance, health insurance, you are the first call they make. If another agent comes along and tries to sell them, they will politely decline the offer and contact you instead.

Now you have expanded the relationship and your customer is referring all their friends...IF the friend asks who they recommend for insurance. Now the last step in my "Prospect Seduction Ladder".

Step #10: Ideal Customer

When I am doing consulting, and I ask the question who is your target market, I often get the description of an Ideal Customer. My new client will typically describe their target market as someone who does not typically shop around, someone that is looking for a business to prescribe a solution for them, someone who listens well, wants and responds to the benefits this business provides.

What my new client does not understand is that he or she has not described a target market but a developed ideal customer. That developed ideal client requires all of the above 9 steps to reach the "Ideal Client" stage. You cannot go out and find a list of more "Ideal Clients" to market your products.

What that business owner asking me for help wants is to just jump from step #1 to Step #10 without any of the hard work required. That isn't possible and causes many new business owners to become frustrated and give up.

Once you have moved the customer through the above 9 steps and created the "Ideal Customer", you understand their business, their personal needs, what motivates them and what will cause the customer to respond.

You will have developed a business relationship on multiple levels. Your customer will be enjoying working with you and will come to you for answers about anything that relates to your business and even some things that don't.

You and your business have become the **Trusted Advisor**. At this stage, you can often move the customer from just providing referrals to endorsed marketing to their friends and/or customers. In this stage, you are often able to get them to send a recommendation letter (that you have composed for them) to their customers or friends recommending you and your business.

Isn't that cool? The "10 Step Sales Seduction Process" begins again but is much easier than starting with a "Luke-Warm Who" list as in Step #1. You are even able to skip the first two or three steps.

You have now entered the realm of successful "Seductive Marketing".

You have developed your customer along a planned line of seduction and they did not even realize they were participating. Isn't that what any single woman would want...and probably even married women from their own husbands.

This is as good as it gets and it only arrives in your lap with a well planned, specifically choreographed system of steps. This is explained better than I have ever seen it done in the book *"Uncensored Sales Strategies"* . . . co-authored by Sydney Biddle Barrows and Dan Kennedy. I recommend you study it in detail and implement the strategies in your business. AND, on top of that, it's a FUN read.

You may be saying to yourself, "this sounds like a lot of work." Yes, there is work involved. If you want a substantial, growing business, it will always require work. But that work will pay off in a rich vein of gold in your business and make it worth 5 or 10 times its current market value.

Now, none of this "Seduction Marketing" means you should consider having sex with your customers. That is a no-no. I am talking about taking them down a path that the prospect doesn't even notice.....that piles on mountains of value in the mind of the prospect, then customer.

That is the real power of "**The 10 Step Prospect Seduction Ladder**".

Chapter Thirteen

Everyone Is In Direct Sales

E VERYONE is in the direct sales business one way or another. Whether you are a "business owner" or an "employee", you are in direct sales. Because no business survives without sales of products or services, it is your number one job as a business owner.

If sales is the number one job, why do business owners often have poor closing ratios?

As I related earlier, for a couple of years, I owned a minority interest in a billboard media company. I had been asked to come in and help the owner of the company revive the business with my marketing coaching and consulting skills.

He had birthed the company four years earlier and it was struggling. The first element of his business that he wanted fixed was an improved salesperson hiring system.

Over the year before I came in, he had hired three different salespeople and given them a base salary plus commission. All three had cost him more than the business they brought in.

He had hired salespeople because he did not enjoy going out and knocking on doors to find prospects. So he decided he would just hire that skill.

One of the Grand Canyon deep misjudgments I see a typical business owner conger up is thinking he can just go out and hire a salesperson and solve all their customer acquisition problems.

The truth is hiring a successful salesperson with the natural skills to suddenly turn your sales around is almost impossible. If you could find someone with that ability, you would have to pay them way to much. The average business owner couldn't afford him or her.

<u>YOU</u> Must Become
Good At Sales First

Since it is difficult and expensive to find a self-starter salesperson with great prospecting and closing skills, you (the average business owner) must become good at selling.

Once you have created, tested, proven and scripted a successful sales system for your business, you can hire salespeople that will use that repeatable system.

With a well crafted, successful selling system, you can hire affordable mediocre sales people, train them and give them the tools to go out and have success. If you are unable to successfully sell your customers with a high percentage close ratio with your passion for your company, why do you think a hired sales person will be able to do it?

What is the top reason most business owners and salespeople do not have a higher closing percentage? Think for a moment. You must have an opinion.

Sales Skills Are Critical To Your Success

I invested 23 years in the corporate sales world as a salesman and sales manager. Most of that time I worked for Fortune 500 companies selling technology products to other Fortune 500 companies. That almost sounds incestuous doesn't it?

One of the great advantages of working in that environment was the high level and expensive sales training I received as part of my job.

By the way, just because it was often expensive did not necessarily make it high level. Often, someone did a first-class sales job on our company's senior management, contracted for a high fee to teach a sales seminar, and then delivered mediocre training. (That can be a lesson to you. You don't always have to have the best product or the most efficient product or service to have success.)

I received tons and tons of training. I had
- ✓ training on consultative selling,
- ✓ training on using questions to sell,
- ✓ training on how to overcome objections,
- ✓ training on negotiating skills,
- ✓ training on selling at a board room level,
- ✓ training in closing techniques,
- ✓ training on connecting with the prospect by mirroring the words they used, the way they sat, the hand gestures they used,
- ✓ and training on how to change my personality style to coincide with that of the person I was selling.

135

They taught me to how to uncover what the person's personality quadrant was. Then having been taught the traits of that type personality I could mold what I said and the way I communicated with them to make the prospect more comfortable with my selling style and like me better.

Why Isn't The Closing Ratio Higher?

Remember the question I started with? Why is it that most business owners and salespeople fail to get a higher closing ratio? The answer I get the most is: "they need more persistence and a better set of words to use at the closing moment to magically get the customer to say yes."

One of the training sessions I attended in my corporate sales years was "The Art of Closing the Sale". The sales professor had a whole two-day course on the top 72 closing techniques and phrases.

If we would just memorize these 72 closing techniques and learn how to use them naturally, we would start seeing a major league increase in our sales totals.

Of course this made the assumption that a salesperson could even remember 72 different sets of phrases to be used at that...most Perfect Moment in Sales...the moment when every prospect is ripe. They just need a little push over the top to get the coveted, YES close from the client. If we just knew the perfect words to say at the perfect time under the perfect conditions, it would be like taking candy from a baby.

I never understood that phrase, "like taking candy from a baby." You try it. If you take candy from a young child; you are in for the worst screaming fit of your life. That does not sound pleasant at all. Is that what I'm going to get from a prospect when I use the perfect close on them and manipulate the prospect into saying yes to my proposition, a crying screaming baby? That is definitely not my idea of a dream selling situation.

Do you know what the biggest problem with the 72 Perfect Closes training is? They are placing way too much emphasis on the moment we ask the person or company to do business with us. The truth that I have learned from what seems like a hundred years of selling experience, I know, I know, it has only been 38 years.

The truth I have learned from all those back-breaking years is: the sale should happen way before the close. The most successful selling happens even before you are in front of the customer or client to ask them to move forward and buy your product or sign up for your service.

So, how do we increase our sales closing percentages? How do we get more customers or clients to do business with us? I will get to that in a moment.

But first, the methods I am reviewing for you in this chapter work not only in face to face selling, like I did for 23 years in corporate technology sales, but also in direct response sales.

In direct response sales, you may use any number of media like direct mail, TV, radio, websites, etc. to close a sale and get someone to order from you or take some action you want without a physical face-to-face contact.

Face To Face Selling

There are advantages to both types of selling. Most "brick and mortar businesses" are in some way involved in ultimately selling face to face.

A smart entrepreneur is developing leads and warm prospects using mass media but he is seldom asking them to make a decision without a face to face contact.

The big advantage provided by face to face selling is your ability to observe body language and facial expressions. You get feedback from the person you are selling. With that feedback, you can adjust what you are saying and demonstrating or even make a decision to leave and not waste any more time based on the body language and the voice intonation used by your prospect.

The leverage given us by mass media is the advantage of speaking to masses of people at the same time and the savings in time that affords us.

The one media where you can combine the advantages of both mass media and visual feedback is speaking. That is the reason I often recommend business owners find a way to gather groups of people together and use a speaking opportunity to deliver the sales presentation to them in groups.

I see this used all the time with financial advisors and insurance agents. They may invite everyone to a lunch, dinner or simple seminar and teach the prospects in the room some interesting, little known secrets and then unveil whatever they are selling as a part of the presentation.

In group selling from the stage, you get the advantages of selling one on many and you get some feedback from the audience as they react to what you are selling.

The opportunity to craft the perfect presentation of your products or service and everyone hears exactly the same most perfect presentation is the BIG advantage in group selling.

With face-to-face selling, you will often make the presentation differently every time you do it. You walk away from it saying to yourself: "Oh, I forgot to tell them this. Or, I wish I had told them that. I now remember exactly the way I should have handled that objection." With group direct response marketing, you have time to write it out and craft the words perfectly to get the best response.

Now, MY answer to the question: Top Reason People Have a Poor Closing Ratio.

Most sales people and business owners place all of the weight for closing the sale on the face to face presentation and the "closing words" that are used. And, little or no emphasis is placed on what the contact knows or believes about you and your product before you arrive for the final closing contact.

Eight Controlling Factors
In Closing the Sale

So how do we significantly improve our odds of getting the prospect to say yes by placing more emphasis on what they know before the sale?

I have "8 Closing the Sale Control Factors" for creating the highest likelihood of getting the sale.

Control Factor #1: List Selection

The first "Control Factor" is List Selection or what my mentor, Dan Kennedy, calls the Who. And no, I'm not talking about those funny little people in "The Grinch Stole Christmas" story and movie. I'm talking about the "WHO" you choose to go after to sell your products. While this seems to be most obvious, it is the step I see missing most in the businesses I help.

Awhile back, I had a consulting appointment with a person that was selling group legal services to companies. The companies she called on could utilize her products as an employee benefit. If an employee had a legal problem he/she had a group of attorneys to call and get help for free.

A Faulty Selling Strategy

The marketing plan she had developed was to go out to office complexes and knock on every door and ask for an appointment to sell this particular service.

She was having lousy closing results. I asked her to consider the following question. Of all the companies that you have sold this service going door to door, what are some common characteristics? She gave me several. I then asked her what percentage of the doors she knocked on had similar characteristics? She felt it was less than 10%.

You see, she had already handicapped her closing ratio because most of the people she was contacting had no propensity to say yes to what she was offering. Ninety percent of these cold prospects didn't have any problems going on in their life or business life that would cause them to be likely candidates for her product.

How much more time, effort and marketing investment could she apply to the prospect if every person she went to see were in that 10%? What if they were all businesses that had events and conditions going on in the business that would make them more likely to respond to her offer? Ninety percent of the people she was contacting were a lousy fit for her services. That was a terrible waste of her time. And time is money, right?

Way too many of the business owners and sales professionals I speak to are in the mode of "anyone with a pulse should pay attention to me and if I just say the right words to convince them they will buy."

Most business owners believe they should open the doors as wide as possible so they do not miss any opportunity to close a sale. When most of the time your likelihood of closing a sale may be less than one in 1,000. Or even if it were 1 in 100, do you have the time to see 100 people to get one sale?

Most business owners are afraid to build smaller marketing entrance doors to their business. Most don't understand the value of investing more money on a smaller number of prospects in order to get a better closing percentage and a higher return-on-investment (ROI).

They want to spend less money per prospect on a larger universe HOPING for a response.

Wayne's Rule
HOPE is a terrible marketing strategy

Wasting Time & Money
On Lousy Prospects

Many of the business owners I see in the market-place are not willing to invest more money to buy a better quality lead, to then get an appointment and a sale.

Most business owners waste too much money and time trying to get a warm lead from very poor prospects. A monumental mistake I see small business owners make is using 50% off discount companies like Groupon to acquire customers.

For most brick and mortar businesses the "Groupon Strategy" attracts mostly the wrong type of customers. Customers attracted to Groupon type coupons seldom build a substantial business. I do not have time or space here to go into why this is a failing strategy for most businesses, but you can ask me sometime in the future in one of my seminars.

I once heard the story of a business owner in the financial services industry that attracts investors to seminars in order to sell to them (speaking from the front of the room). This business owner was running an extensive test using big broad ads in the newspaper and direct mail to particular zip codes of affluence, attracting investors to his seminars.

He also decided to test targeting ONLY prospects known to own annuities. The cost of putting the annuity investors in the room was three times as high as the general population group he had been attracting. However, the NET Profit from the seminar even after higher cost of putting them in the seats was double when he put people in the room who were known to own annuities vs. a broad brush audience in the room.

This verifies the principal that a "buyer is a buyer is a buyer". You can take a salesperson with the same presentation, the same skill, the same offer and put them in front of two very different sourced prospects or groups of prospects and get two very different closing outcomes.

If I Only Knew Then What I Know Now

When I owned a Commercial Lease Consulting company back in the 90's, I was working with companies that were leasing space from a commercial landlord.

I would contact everyone within an area that didn't own the building they were in. I would wait for a response and go do an audit of their lease and find discrepancies and overbilling that we would get refunded to the tenant. If I knew then what I know now, I would have concentrated my efforts and spent more money marketing to smaller locally owned businesses renting from retail strip centers and shopping malls. Looking back, that is where most of my best and most lucrative clients developed.

Bill Glazer, author of the book *"Outrageous Advertising That Is Outrageously Successful"*, sells business building information products to owners of small retail businesses teaching them how to increase their sales.

He found that his lifetime profit per client is higher from female business owners. He says he is now investing more money and getting a higher marketing ROI selling to retail businesses that have an owner's first name that appears to be a woman.

In our economy, the cost per sale is going up. And having customers and warm prospects that are more likely to spend more money with you is a critical asset to have going forward. Consequently, the result you get at the end of your sales process is often more dependent on Who you are in front of at the beginning of the process than the sales skills you employ.

Who you pick to present your product to at the beginning and how much you are able to spend on getting them to respond, significantly affects the outcome at the end. So our first "Closing the Sale Control Factor" is the list of prospects you choose in the very beginning. I have a key strategy that I use with clients to quickly and easily create this best prospect definition.

Control Factor #2: How Relevant Is Your Product or Service to the Group You Have Chosen

This is closely related to Number 1. It is often perplexing when I talk to professional sales people about a prospect they are about to go see and they haven't even Googled the name of the prospect or the business.

Number two is about how you customize the message for selling your product or service to the prospect list you have chosen in number one.

The more you know about the prospects chosen in Number 1; the more you can make your product or service, your proof, your message, relevant to that particular person's interests and belief system. This is why the vast majority of mass market large corporation brand oriented advertising is so hard to make work. The advertising message isn't relevant to the audience that is seeing or hearing the message. There is massive waste as a result.

There are high quality magazines that I read with ads for very expensive watches. I have little or no interest in very expensive watches. I fear that I might be walking down Central Avenue one day and someone will come along and cut off my hand to steal my expensive watch to sell and get drugs. The watch advertisers in these magazines are not making it relevant to me.

I once saw an ad for a generic brand of vitamins that promote healthier eyes and help you focus better at long distances. This particular ad was in the National Rifle Association magazine of all places. The vitamins were a very generic product but the ad was specifically crafted to sell to gun owners. There is nothing special about the vitamins the company was advertising. You could buy these vitamins at any Walgreens store.

If sold like most would sell it, the advertiser would just talk about the vitamins being great for your eyes and improving sight. But this ad targeted the audience of this publication who own rifles and like to hunt big game. It was all about hunting and marksmanship. It has a message that would resonate with the readers of the NRA magazine. This advertisement gets more attention and sells more vitamins because the seller has made it relevant to the chosen audience. The seller has identified who would have a higher propensity to want to solve the problem that this product solves.

If a generic ad for this product were published in a general interest magazine that these same people also read, the company would get little or no response from these hunters. That poor result is because the hunter would not see a message that would be relevant to them, that would cause a response. But this ad gets response. It is made relevant to the hunter's situation and belief system. By the way, I saw an ad for the same vitamins in the Airline Pilots and Aircraft Owners Magazine. Its message was focused on the distant clear vision problems experienced in flying an airplane.

If you want real success in your business you must first stop throwing mud against a wall and HOPING! Instead, craft special messages to smaller target avatars that make your product or service relevant to that market. Then you get higher success in closing and better response from your audience.

Wayne's Rule
Stop throwing mud against the wall and start Target Marketing for best results.

Your closing ratio will skyrocket simply because you have crafted the message of your product or service specifically for me your prospect. I will respond because it is relevant to how I see the world, my beliefs, my needs and my wants.

This way you are selling what appears to be a custom product specifically designed for me rather than a general product.

Control Factor #3: Pre-Sales Positioning

How you position yourself and your company before you go in for the sale is a critical element in the sales process. Remember, closing the sale is more a Process than an Event. You should first position yourself as a trusted advisor not as a salesperson. You want prospects to perceive you and your company as someone who provides little known, valuable information to the prospect, as being a consultant or providing diagnostic information to them.

This is no different whether you are selling a specialized product or service or a commodity. There are always things that you know that your customer doesn't know and will value from you if they are provided the information. I talked about the value of information marketing in any business earlier in this book.

Here is an example of the implementation of this concept in a commodity type business here in Albuquerque.

One of my clients was the owner of local auto repair shop. You cannot get much more commodity than that. Everybody and their brother owns an auto repair shop. Everyone is competing on lower prices until hardly anyone is making any profit in the business.

This owner explained how he tells people they are welcome to call either of his two shops for a consultation on how they can fix their own car and whether the customer should consider the problem serious or not. He teaches them through his newsletter how to do some of their own auto maintenance.

As a result, when they come to him with a problem, they are already sold that he is the Doctor of Auto Repair and Service and they should take whatever prescription he is delivering for them. Because of what he does in advance, he seldom gets the complaint – "that costs too much".

By the time his prospects/customers need the car repaired, they are convinced he has their best interest at heart and would not recommend something unless it is vital to the health of their automobile. Who wants to be driving around in the heat of New Mexico with a sick automobile? He has the prescription.

Get Out Of the Commodity Business

Many people tell me they are in a commodity business and people will choose to go down the street for a cheaper price. They are often very right because the only differentiation the prospect sees in the competing businesses is price.

Most car owners do not have any idea what is going on when a problem develops with their car. You call most repair shops, they will tell you to just bring it in and they will fix it for you.

But our smart "Authority Level Business Owner" provides a higher level of valued service. He provides this consultation service and provides a constant flow of information that teaches people about maintaining their car. They trust him because he gives them free training.

At sometime a light, on the dashboard of the car of one of his customers, may come on and stay on. The owner fears what it might mean and panics. The customer or prospect calls my client's shops for a consultation and finds out (after a couple of questions) the light was just warning them they had forgotten to close the gas tank lid tight enough. That saves them the wasted time of a trip to the garage and keeps them from spending wasted money.

The average auto repair shop would take that opportunity to find a reason to sell them repairs they don't really need. In my client's case, after saving them a costly repair, the prospect or customer now trusts the repair shop and the owner. Also the owner is able to use these calls to turn 30% of them into revenue generating repairs. He may not have had that chance if he had not offered the free telephone consultation.

The truth is; most local businesses are in a commodity business. Almost always someone else around the corner sells the same kinds of products or services you sell. Many of them are selling it cheaper. If not today, they will be at some time in the future. Your competition is or will be selling at lower prices, because the only response most business owners have to slow sales is dropping the price to make more sales.

I do not have time to go into it in this book, but that is a losing proposition that will drive you into bankruptcy and closing your business. You must make a profit. Lowering the price to get more sales cuts profit fast and is a losing proposition for everyone.

Position as the Expert Authority

Proper positioning is the one ingredient that can set your business apart from everyone else. Manufacturing you as a credible expert, authority figure, trusted advisor or celebrity is the optimum way to change your positioning in the marketplace and get you a reasonable price for your products.

Trusted advisor or celebrity status is the primary reason some doctors can charge huge fees while others doing the same work are limited to whatever crumbs the insurance companies are willing to hand out. Your Utopian Position is the combination of all four. By the way, the most powerful of these is being viewed as a celebrity in your industry. It is far more effective for positioning than just being the expert.

I'm not talking about becoming a Hollywood actor or Snookie from Jersey Shore. All you need is your prospects and customers viewing you as the celebrity in your particular industry. That can be created by things like writing a book on your industry or being interviewed on radio or TV, etc.

To create the best of all worlds, become the Celebrity Expert in your industry. Then people will take your prescription without argument. The customer will just do whatever you tell them to do.

The prospect or customer will stop haggling over price for fear you would not accept them as a client. If they don't accept your prescription and price, they will miss out on an extremely valuable relationship. That is the positioning you must develop for yourself in some way.

A local heart doctor here in Albuquerque is on the morning TV news program a couple of times a week. He spends about 3-4 minutes answering questions and giving advice about general medical topics.

Because he is on TV as The Expert, his patients pay more to see and be treated by him for heart ailments than most any of the other heart doctors in town. He is not necessarily any better than the other heart doctors. He may not even be as good. I don't know.

But because he is the celebrity doctor on TV dispensing education about how people can improve their health and use medical treatments properly, he is the overwhelming choice for people who can afford to pay for the best.

Set Up the Sale In Advance

A major part of your presale positioning is setting up the sale so the prospect is convinced in advance they are going to be damn lucky to get to do business with you.

Once you decide what the positioning you want to achieve looks like, you should consider all of the various tools that will allow you to accomplish this positioning in the prospect's mind. It may be authoring a book. It may be hiring a bigger name celebrity to co-author a book with you or act as your advertising spokesperson. It may be doing lectures and speaking appearances. It may be writing articles for your local paper.

Certainly, the most important devices are what you put into the hands of your prospect between the time they step forward and identify themselves as a potential lead and the time that a sales presentation is given and a sale created.

For instance, a carpet cleaning company coming in for the first time might give the client a DVD to view before the sales presentation is given and the price is discussed.

This DVD might:

- Explain all the health risks and allergy related problems caused by contaminates in the carpet.

- Show the prospect scientific research that backs up the claim.
- Explain the special system used by the carpet cleaner to remove these contaminates better than the average carpet cleaner.
- Show a short clip of the owner being interviewed on TV.
- Demonstrate the reason the carpet cleaner does testing on the carpet and how they remove the stains.
- Explain the special equipment the carpet cleaner uses to get the best results.
- Show a graphic of a book the owner has written on household contaminates and their effects and offer to give them a copy with their cleaning.

Increasing Your Closing Ratio

To make closing the sale easier, you must differentiate yourself and your business.

One of the devices I discussed earlier and that I use with clients to accomplish this differentiation from the competition is the "Knock Their Socks Off Package." This device is a way to really change your positioning when you feel you are in a commodity business.

In the speaking for hire business, most speakers receiving an inquiry from a speaking opportunity would send a fancy brochure and maybe a CD or an example video of one of their speeches. A demo tape if you will. And if the speaker had written a book, it was included. That was it.

A few years back, there was a corporate speaker by the name of Larry Dolan that succeeded in getting 80% of his inquiries to book him to speak. He would take a box like you would get envelopes in from the office supply house. He would fill that box with photocopies of testimonial letters from people who had hired him to speak in the past.

Out of this stack of testimonial letters, he would choose the ones that had some relationship to the audience for this engagement. If it was from the automotive industry he would put letters from people in the automobile business. If it was small business owners, it would be small business association letters. He would take these chosen letters and put them on top of the stack.

Now, I doubt anyone ever went through all the testimonial letters. But the sheer number by itself "Knocked Their Socks Off" and caused the event coordinator to feel Larry would be a successful choice for the event.

The speaker would "packing tape" the box together and FedEx it to a meeting planner. He refused to send a threefold brochure. He refused to send a demo tape. He just sent a box full of satisfied clients.

That was his "Knock Their Socks Off Package". The fact that it was different from anything anyone else was sending. And the sheer size when it was delivered to the meeting planner's office caused it to have impact. The fact that it was sent FedEx had impact. All this gave him enormous credibility and competitive advantage prior to ever talking to the event coordinator about booking the speaking opportunity.

Shed Shop Example

An example of a different "Knock Their Socks Off Package" that Dan Kennedy designed for a client is one I show in my "Small Business Marketing 101 Workshop". We study it in more detail in my MasterMind groups. It is Dan's Shed Shop example.

Dan had a client selling pre-built backyard wooden sheds. THAT is definitely a commodity business. Everyone else in the industry normally sent the prospect a fancy brochure listing all the sizes and prices of their sheds.

Dan had the Shed Shop send a DVD in an infomercial format showing stories of happy shed shop owners using their sheds in different ways. And of course at least one of the stories included an older lady shedding tears about the difference it had made in her life.

The shed shop's "Knock Their Socks Off Package" also included a booklet of 102 stories of shed shop owners with photos showing all the different ways people were using their sheds to make their life better.

It included literature with photos of all the many additional features a prospect could add to his or her shed to make it more custom designed for the owner. The Shed Shop even added in a list of questions a prospect should ask any company selling sheds.

Nobody else did anything close to this. The Shed Shop manufacturer was able to sell at prices 40 - 50% higher than anyone else. Purely by employing this "Knock Their Socks Off" package of information, it resulted in his company going from about a 30% first call close rate to just under an 80% first call close rate.

When the Shed Shop salesperson arrived, the homeowner was already convinced this was the company they wanted to build and deliver their shed. This was accomplished just by setting up the customer's expectation by the significant difference in what they received in advance of the sale. A hidden significant advantage was in changing the purpose of the customer's purchase from buying additional backyard storage to buying a special purpose bonus room in the back yard.

They were now buying a playhouse for the kids, or craft room, or artist studio. After viewing this package, the prospect stopped just looking for storage. The Shed Shop owner had demonstrated (through his "Knock Their Socks Off Package") that a wooden shed was much more than storage.

This small business, high power, marketing strategy is designed to create an eye opening experience and significantly raise the value of the business in the prospect's eyes because of its elaborateness, the bulk, and its means of delivery.

The content of your "Knock Their Socks Off Package" is specifically designed to position your business head-and-shoulders above the competition by the time the prospect takes the "Next Step" you recommend. That "Next Step" could be either inviting the salesperson into their home or office, or going to the company's office, show-room, doctor's office or whatever.

Takes Price Out of the Decision

The customer is now as close to predetermined to do business with you and buying your product or service as you can get. He is very unlikely to challenge your prescription, your solution or your price.

Go do some research and look at what the other businesses in your industry are sending to their warm prospects, people who have responded with interest. Finding a way to send something of perceived value, that is significantly more than your competition, will separate you from them in the prospect's mind.

Prospects will be attracted to you and your business. They will stop being skeptical of you as just another salesperson. They will stop being as price sensitive and you can stop saying, "everyone just wants the cheapest price".

Now that is "Pre-Sales Positioning".

Control Factor #4: The Belief or Disbelief In Your Value Statements

This speaks to the credibility issue of your presentation. What the prospect receives from you in advance of your closing call helps with this belief about what you say. If you ever have an unsatisfactory closing ratio or find closing sales difficult, it probably means your claims have not been believed by the prospect along the way.

This is not solved by adding a cleverer close, or 5 bonuses to the close. The answer is found in going back through your sales process all the way from the point someone raises their hand through to the final sales presentation. Take a look at every instance in which you are asking the prospect to accept something as fact. Then analyze how well you frame and prove the statement so the prospect will accept and believe it.

In the old Encyclopedia Britannica sales business, the Director of Marketing that was responsible for hiring sales people to go out into people's homes and sell the encyclopedias discovered that if he hired and sent in a school teacher the closing ratio was higher.

Why were school teachers better closers? It wasn't because they had better closing skills. It turned out that identifying themselves as teachers lent immediate credibility to the importance of having these learning books in the home to improve their child's educational achievement. The teacher salesperson had greater credibility and overcame the prospect's disbelief because of who they were.

The truth was that teachers were not natural salespeople. It took a whole lot more expense and effort to train a teacher to sell. But, because of who they were, they overcame the natural reluctance a prospect has in believing the salesperson. Even when there are obvious reasons not to believe the salesperson, you can overcome that with the right person and the right message.

Victor Kiam and the Remington Shaver

Another example is when Victor Kiam bought the Remington shaver company. He was one of the first CEOs to do commercials for his own company. But by his positioning statement he was able to change the argument.

He would say the following in his commercials. "I liked the shaver so much that I bought the company." The truth was, he owned the company so he HAD TO LIKE the shaver. But by forming the statement this way, he took away the argument that he had to like the shaver because he was the owner. It made the whole commercial more believable.

You can see this in infomercials on TV where a celebrity spokesperson will say, "I liked this product so much I wanted to be the spokesperson for it." That statement makes the celebrity and their assertions about the product much more believable and less like a paid talking head.

Guarantees Increase Believability

There are many other ways to make your claims believable. The promise of high value from one of my workshops is hard to prove believable. One of the methods I use is our Guarantee.

"If you attend the workshop and don't hear at least two ideas that will pay for the workshop 10 times over, just tell us so and we will refund your money, give you $250 for your time AND you get to keep all of the handout materials."

We did something similar in my website catalog company. It is hard to know if the quality of a fabric product like a comforter ensemble or bedspread is going to meet your expectation when all you get to see is a photo on the internet. Our website told them that we only choose the best quality products. But how do we prove it to them? How do we make it believable from such a great distance?

We did it with the longest guarantee in our industry (not longest in words...longest in time). The standard guarantee on the internet was 30 days, many times plus a restocking fee.

"Keep it for 90 days, if you aren't happy with your choice for any reason (you can even use the "dog ate my reason" excuse), you may return it for a full refund and WE will pay for the return shipping. That's how good our quality and service is."

Customer Testimonial Evidence

You should be using customer testimonials as convincing evidence of your assertions.

Wayne's Rule
What your customers say about your business is significantly more believable than what you say about your business even if you are far better at saying it.

Here is a testimonial example from one of my past Platinum MasterMind members.

"I would like to take a moment to thank you for the difference you have made in my life and my business! I had attended your PowerCircle™ meetings regularly and would get very excited about the new things I would learn, but I had such a hard time actually implementing them in my business. So I took a HUGE step and joined your MasterMind group. I wasn't sure if I could afford it, but I soon found out I could not afford not to be part of your MasterMind group. It is easy to see how I can apply the marketing teachings to everyone else's business. Being part of your MasterMind group has helped me understand how to put the marketing strategies into my own business. It also helped me in many other ways I did not expect, such as: hiring and training employees, building systems in my agency and identifying exactly who my clients are. It has made me thousands of dollars and saved me thousands of dollars! It has also given me other ideas of how I can expand my business, in ways I would have never imagined. I was the #1 agent of new business sales for my district, the same year we had 3 rate increases. Everyone wants to know what I do different. I am asked to speak regularly to new agents that join our company to help them grow their agency. Last but not least the relationships I have built with the others in our group are PRICELESS! Once again, thank you for inviting me into your select group of successful business owners!"
Jo Medina, The Medina Agency, Albuquerque, NM

You should be using testimonials in everything that goes out to your prospects and customers. I use testimonials in my newsletter every month. When I send a sales letter selling one of my workshops or our

PowerCircle, I always include testimonials. The inclusion of testimonials is my best way to create believability.

Control Factor #5: The prospect's belief or disbelief in THEIR ability to use your product or service

Number 4 was the belief or disbelief that the prospect has about what you say about your product or service. In other words do they believe what YOU say?

Number 5 is about the prospect's skepticism that your product or service will do for HIM or HER what you say it will do. Salespeople and lawyers will say anything to get what they want, right? I know the world thinks salespeople are a little higher on the credibility scale than lawyers . . . but not much!

Your prospect may well believe what you are saying is true for others, but does he, the prospect, believe he can actually get the product or service to work for him?

Your prospect may believe in your product. He may believe what you say is true, but he doesn't believe in himself — that HE can use the product or service successfully. The prospect is sometimes afraid it will just sit on the shelf unused.

Number 5 is one of the least understood of these eight. A lot of emphasis in marketing and selling is put on No. 4, getting them to believe what you say. But many do not understand that No. 5 may be much more important.

For instance in the infomercial advertising business, a lot of emphasis and commercial design is placed on the physical demonstration. They work a lot on showing how the thing works and does everything they say through visual demonstration.

When you watch an infomercial for a kitchen gadget for instance, they demonstrate it. They show that it cuts tomatoes 17 different ways and makes cute little designs with them. The infomercial will use scientific data drawn from Wall Street Journal. On and on and on — they substantiate all of the claims they are making about the slicer/dicer gadget.

Prospects Often Do Not Believe In Themselves

There is a key factor about human nature that many business owners and marketers do not understand. The prospect can accept all of what you say and demonstrate and still not buy, because of their own self image, their own past experience, and their own beliefs about themselves. They don't believe that THEY can successfully use the product or get value out of the service.

For example, I am often selling information products that help a business owner grow the business, or a workshop or seminar to teach business owners and sales professionals how to get more customers and make more money more quickly.

If my prospect knows that they have bought 28 other programs or DVD learning sets and they are all on the bookshelf with the shrink wrap still on them, and I ignore this, I am going to fail to make the sale. Because that person in his heart knows that he will not get around to using it. And, if I did not do something to convince him otherwise, there will be no sale. Are you doing this in your business?

In selling diet products, you may get someone to believe that it works, that it works for other people just like them. They might even believe that it works for people of their gender or of their race or ethnicity, age, occupation, in their town. But if they have failed 6 other times on 6 other products or diet systems, they will not respond.

People tend to disqualify themselves. They will find reasons why, even though it works and works for others, it will not work for them.

Now, let's go back to the kitchen gadget show. There was a guy in the infomercial business for years, Stan Jacobs that was a specialist in doing demonstration shows.

Stan said, "It's one thing to have a great professional demonstrator demo the gadget. But, the most successful demonstration happens when you have a live audience and you pick someone out of the audience, bring them up to the kitchen counter and have THEM use it. And low and behold they ARE able to use it just as easily as the demonstrator."

This is something a lot of salespeople, a lot of marketers, just DO NOT understand. The final obstacle to the close is not the belief the prospect has in the product or the service, its features or benefits, but the prospect's belief in one's self. "Can I successfully use it?"

Here is a short list of ways you can help your prospects believe they will be able to use the product or service themselves like you say.

- One is testimonials. And not just one or two testimonials, but an overwhelming number of testimonials.
- Awards that you have won and recognition you've been given as the expert through interviews on TV or radio or written by you or about you in a book.
- Your personal story can be used if you can make it relevant by setting up how even someone like

you can do it. Your story must relate to how you are like the buyer and you were able to do it so they can do it.

I demonstrate the "Personal Story" method in one of my marketing training workshop with an advertisement that has run in national high-end investment magazines like Investor's Business Daily for a number of years with the headline:

Former Iowa Prison Guard Shows Frustrated Investors How To Escape From Financial Prison And Truly Profit From America's Heartland!

If someone as low on the totem pole as an Iowa prison guard can find the secret and be successful at investing in commercial properties in "America's Heartland" (Iowa) even I can do it.

You can also add an iron clad more than money back guarantee that demonstrate your belief they can succeed or it will cost you money (not just return the prospect's money).

But whatever you do, you must give the prospect significant reasons to believe he or she will be able to succeed or be pleased with your product or service.

You must in some way help your prospect demonstrate to himself, that he can actually get it to work.

Control Factor #6: Structure of the Offer

Most bricks and mortar business owners are doing a poor job of this. You must position offers in front of your prospects that are easy for them to take action and easy to understand.

This is a mistake that is often made in face to face selling or from the front of the room selling. Many, many times the prospect is so confused at the end of your advertisement about how he is supposed to take action and what he is getting that nothing happens.

This is a problem that I work on constantly in our PowerCircle™ meetings. What are the words I can use in our offer (for guests to join PowerCircle™), that are easy to understand and makes it easy for the guests to take action. My monthly free "Small Business Customer Vortex Workshop™"' is an additional step in the sales process to help me accomplish this.

The way I present the offer to join and when I present it in the PowerCircle™ meeting and again in the workshop is being adjusted and tracked to see when the best results happen.

In one of his newsletter articles, Dan Kennedy tells the example of the client that he helped get an infomercial designed and developed for a "Gold by the Inch" business. The infomercial's magic was that you quickly and easily understood what this thing was, how it worked and what you were being asked to do.

"Gold by the Inch" was a business opportunity. There were many ways to sell the product but the key play was to have multiple spools of different gold chains and set the spools up on a card table at a swap meet. People would walk up and get a bracelet or anklet cut and custom designed on the spot. The buyer would be paying by the inch not by the piece.

The infomercial showed business owners sitting at a swap meet with chains on the table. People were walking up and asking what this was, getting a simple answer, picking a design of the chain, chain pulled off, snipped, fastener put on and the customer handing the business owner money.

The viewer immediately understood how the business worked and made money. The infomercial wasn't asking anyone to do something that a fairly talented chimpanzee couldn't do. The prospect watching the infomercial could see themselves doing it. There was instant understanding. The offer itself was easy because it was a free lead generation offer. Then the subsequent offers were easy also. You were only picking between three choices that were easy to understand.

There is a great book by Barry Swartz titled "The Paradox of Choice". The author lays out examples and scientific research that make the point that in many cases we have basically reached the place that consumers have too many choices. Prospects are paralyzed in this advertising saturated world. They are unable to choose.

So it is important for us to make it easy for the prospect to make a choice. If your offer is too complicated, if it is difficult to choose, it naturally lends itself to the "I need to think it over" response; "I need to sleep on it;" or, the "I need to talk it over with someone else" reaction.

That response immediately derails our close.

Often we give the prospect only one way to respond. However, I have found better response if I make it easier to respond by giving him or her two or three response choices.

For instance:
- Go to a website and order,
- Fax in a registration form,
- Call and order over the phone

Control Factor #7: Risk Reversal

You must eliminate risk completely. If you can find a way to remove all the risk from an offer, and also make them believe they will be successful and happy with your solution to their problem, you've taken away the biggest hurdle in the sale.

Tom Rebar leads a group like our PowerCircle™ group in Green Bay, Wisconsin. His primary business sells in a business-to-business (B2B) environment rather than a business-to-consumer (B2C). Business owners often tell me it is significantly harder to provide risk reversal in B2B sales than it is in B2C selling situations.

Tom sells a system that teaches large companies how to control their inventory. Most of the time, he is not dealing with the owner or a senior executive of the company. He is usually selling to a lower level manager that is responsible for inventory control in the company. *Risk Reversal* is a little different when designed for a manager in the company. In this case, the risk experienced by the middle manager was the potential of being perceived as a poor decision maker in front of the senior executives of the company. He risked looking bad in front of his bosses who could fire him for those poor decisions.

With the B2C prospect or selling directly to the owner of a company, risk reversal is easier to accomplish because the only person that owner or consumer answers to is himself. If they make a bad buying decision, no one else is going to know about it.

Developing a system, for taking away all the risk the prospect feels, makes a significant difference in your closing percentage. When you understand the connection between this #7 and #1 (the choice of the prospect you are selling your product), you begin to realize why this is SO important. A lot of business owners or marketers are very reluctant to construct really great risk elimination or even risk reversal offers.

"Risk Elimination" is making it go away. "Risk Reversal" is actually making it go away plus punishing and penalizing you the seller more than the amount of the refund. Most business owners are afraid to design in "Risk Reversal" because they fear the prospect will take advantage.

One of the ways to help eliminate this fear is to be selling in front of really good qualified prospects in the first place, #1. The better quality the prospect or the customer the less likely they are to abuse or take advantage of the guarantee, the warranty or the risk reversal offer that you put in front of them. The poorer the quality of the prospect, the more likely they are to abuse it. In both B2B and B2C this is reality.

Now, let's get back to my Tom Rebar example. In many cases he was dealing with a lower level manager of a big company whose job is at stake when he makes a bad decision. But for the manager, the upside isn't really there either. When you or I make a decision, there is a financial upside. If we make the right decision we get to take advantage of the upside. But in this particular case this manager is reluctant to take the risk because he doesn't get any value out of the upside. B-U-T, he really gets clobbered on the downside.

Tom was working hard to close a very lucrative sale to a really big company, but he was having a bear of a time penetrating. He did have a guarantee on the training that at the end of the two days if the client wasn't happy with the training they could get their money back.

He finally cracked this company by giving this manager a 3-year wage guarantee. If this goes south on him, and he gets fired, Tom guaranteed he would pay the guy's salary for three years.

You wouldn't dare do this if you were not dealing with a high quality responsible company, a high quality individual in whom you had confidence, AND had high confidence in the product you were selling. But this is a great example of creative risk reversal under the right client quality circumstances.

Here are some standard Risk Reversals that I have used.

"I guarantee you will walk away from our Website Vortex Bootcamp™ with at least three strategies that when implemented will increase the income from your website by at least 20 times the investment in the workshops. If you are not satisfied by the lunch break, we'll refund your tuition plus give you $100 for your time. If we don't wow you, it will cost me money."

My Unheard of 90 Day Money Back Guarantee

At my website catalog company, we took it one step farther with our "**Never Before Heard of Return Policy**".

"Take 90 days to try out your new Southwestern home decor items. If you aren't completely satisfied, call us within 90 days and we'll refund all your money AND pay the return shipping. No Questions Asked - No Hard Feelings."

You see the norm for everyone else in the industry was a 30 day money back guarantee. Many would even charge a 15% restocking fee. We tripled the guarantee time and paid for the shipping both ways. **No one else would do that.** But we took away all of the risk from the new customer. There was nothing to fear. You must find a way to take away all their fear of loss or failure.

By the way, we had an unexpected reward.

Our return rate on orders went from just over 9% down to 3% after implementing the 90 day guarantee. All of my competition laughed at us thinking the refund rate would get worse. THEY WERE WRONG!

Control Factor #8: Unasked Questions and Objections Answered

This is one of the most important copywriting strategies that I learned from Dan. I haven't heard many others talk about this and it is a CRITICAL element in setting up an easy close of the sale. If you miss this step you can leave what I call an "Elephant in the Room" that will crater your sale and you will not know why it happened.

In Dan's copywriting training, he taught me to always bring up the unasked question that will probably be in the mind of the prospect. An interesting example of this is a copywriting example Dan gave us in a rewrite of an Insurance Agent's letter to new movers.

The first sentence leads off:

"I'll bet the last person you want a letter from today is an insurance salesperson."

Isn't that the BIG FAT ELEPHANT in the room when an insurance salesperson comes calling??? Nevertheless, getting it out of the way up-front gives the prospect confidence that this agent understands what he (the prospect) is thinking. It also creates interest when the agent immediately takes the opportunity to explain why this insurance agent is different and valuable to the reader.

Because of the lessons I have learned from Dan, I'm a big proponent of not ignoring any elephant in the room, rather pointing it out and painting it purple.

Most sales people and a lot of copywriters prefer to just keep their fingers crossed and hope that nobody brings up the objection or thinks about it. But I believe that is a mistake. Your customers are a whole lot more sophisticated than that.

AND, because of the economy and the saturation in the number of products and services being sold to consumers, I think your prospects are more skeptical and scared than ever.

I have always followed this rule even in face to face selling. In face to face selling you have the advantage of feedback. So a lot of sales people error in only responding to the questions and objections raised by the prospect. But, there are many reasons your prospect will leave the unasked questions or objections on the table without bringing them up. In most cases, there are more objections on their mind and bothering them. The prospect just is not voicing them to you.

In some cases, they are TOO polite to bring up the objection and cause a confrontation. Sometimes they might be afraid to ask a stupid question because it might make them look dumb or petty. In other cases they do not want to be thought of as cheap or a cheapskate. There are any number of reasons the prospect doesn't bring up every objection.

Address Them or Lose The Sale

When I was selling mainframe computer technology products back in the late 80s, I flew out from Houston to close a big sale to a large grocery store chain here in Albuquerque. I lost the sale because I didn't address one single disadvantage we had in our product.

Our system required a standalone cabinet rather than mounting the equipment in the customer's existing rack system. The customer did not bring it up. And neither did I. In fact, I thought I had dodged the bullet, until later. I found out the prospect company went with my competitor and the reason they gave was the competitor's system would be mounted in their existing data cabinets. It did not require extra computer room floor space. That problem became a big deal to them and my competitor made sure they noticed it. Because I failed to address this "Elephant in the Room" and handle the objection, it became THE reason not to buy our system. AND worse, I lost a really big sale and commission.

You should never make the assumption that merely addressing only the objections raised by the prospect is sufficient to get to a close.

That goes double when crafting sales copy in advertising. You should think of everything that might come up in the prospect's mind, every objection, every anxiety, every reason for not buying and go ahead and lay those out on the table and answer them.

I know it is difficult in a display ad or in a Yellow Pages advertisement. There isn't enough room available to cover objections. That is one of the reasons in display ads for my clients I design in a 2-Step sales process. Instead of trying to jump directly to the sale, I create an offer to send the prospect more information that is designed to help complete the sale. You must put yourself in the information business.

There are many copywriting devices you can use to overcome this potential pit fall in the sales process. You can do it with a frequently asked questions list or by telling stories. You can use testimonials that introduce the issue and answer it from a customer's viewpoint. The mechanics of getting it done are varied. But, the overriding principle is to leave no unasked question unanswered.

I believe business owners and salespeople are fearful of this issue or at least negligent of it. I know I was in my old corporate sales days and it cost me a lot of money.

Usually the small business owner believes, "if Fred doesn't bring it up then for sure I shouldn't mention it. Why introduce another potential objection when the prospect might not be thinking about it." But just because Fred Prospect has not put it on the table in front of you, does not mean it isn't rolling around in Fred's brain.

However, there is a big benefit in fielding objections Fred has not yet asked. Your process of talking about any weaknesses (and handling them) often builds trust. Because you are willing to talk about your negatives as well as your positives, your prospect might think, "You must be more trustworthy of our relationship together. Nobody else tells us what the potential issues are in their products. They leave it to us to find out after it is too late."

These 8 factors are critical to making it easier when we get to the point of asking the prospect to take action. Build these 8 into your sales process and the close happens almost automatically.

Chapter Fourteen

Three Powerful Marketing Content Strategies

Most business owners I meet lack any kind of formal sales training and almost none have any training in crafting and writing compelling sales copy. Consequently, they often miss some of the most compelling strategies for getting the customer to say yes and buy.

There are three very powerful strategies I use in the selling process and for formulating interesting advertising sales copy that significantly improves your ability to convince your prospect to buy the products or services you sell.

Strategy 1:
Change Your Sales Message From Telling Facts to Telling Stories

The use of stories in face-to-face selling and in advertising copy is one of the most powerful and least understood techniques for creating connection with your prospect.

The two most effective types of stories are your own personal story and your customer stories. You can tell how your current customers are using your service or product and getting satisfaction. You can also use the story as an illustration of how the product is solving their problem. The most convincing marketing systems and sales presentations include both types of stories.

We have grown up hearing stories from our parents, grandparents, and the great speakers we've heard. We go to movies and watch TV to hear stories. It is in our nature to believe stories. In the last few years, Hollywood has often used movies and TV shows as a liberal propaganda vehicle...more stories.

At my monthly PowerCircle™ meetings I am constantly telling stories to illustrate the points I am making. I do the same in all the workshops I conduct. They are chocked full of stories. You will hear my personal stories that make a particular point. You have seen many of them in this book. In fact, I started this book with the "Knock Their Socks Off" story.

I carefully craft stories of business owners using the strategies I teach that demonstrate the value of the information. The stories are specifically designed to keep the member, reader or prospect engaged in what I want them to learn and discover.

174

That is the purpose of the use of stories in your sales material and your sales presentations. You need to develop stories to engage your audience. Almost everything you talk about can be presented better in the context of a story and you'll find you have more success when you use them.

Many years ago, there was a very popular TV show called "The Waltons". It was a show about a family living through the great depression years. It told the story of an extended family living together. There were the parents and the 5 or 6 kids, I forget how many. And grandpa and grandma lived with them also.

Frequently, one of the kids would have some great dilemma they were having to live through or something they had done wrong and were in trouble. Almost always, grandpa would sit the child down and tell them a story of when he was young and was faced with this problem and the unique way he dealt with it.

The child and the audience learned the lesson far better from the story than if grandpa had just said this is what you should do.

When you build stories into your sales presentations, you will sell less on facts and more on emotions. And, as my experience of 23 years in corporate sales and over 20 years of small business ownership have proven to me over and over again, prospects almost always buy based on emotional decisions.

Wayne's Rule
Prospects buy on emotion and justify to their friends with your facts

---

The Amazing Power of
Your Personal Story

First, let's start with your Personal Story or Stories. There is bound to be a story that you have lived that:

- ✓ is associated with how and why you got into your business or,
- ✓ demonstrates a compelling reason why you chose this business or,
- ✓ makes you especially suited to be an expert in this business or,
- ✓ caused you to start this business to solve particular customer/client/patient problems, or
- ✓ shows that you are similar to your customers, or
- ✓ multiples of the above.

Your personal story helps you create affinity with your prospects and customers. It also helps validate your expert status that you SHOULD be creating for yourself in your business. Because you know more about your business than any of your customers, you can...right now...go out and declare yourself an expert or specialist. Even if you do not know everything, there is a lot of insider information you DO know about your business that prospects have not discovered yet, b-u-t, if they just knew, they would want to do business with you.

You Are An Expert
Just Prove It With Your Story

You can easily demonstrate expertise with stories about how you started your business and all the research you completed to be able to properly solve the problems of people that need your product or service.

Potential prospects prefer to do business with experts/specialists they can trust. Your prospects want to feel like they are buying from the best in the field. If they are unable to find an expert they will typically fall back on price. Your story connected to your reason for being in business is a very powerful tool that demonstrates you are the expert.

"Birthing My Coaching & Consulting Business" Story

I invested 23 years in selling products and services, mostly in the computer technology business to Fortune 1,000 companies as I worked for Fortune 500 type companies. I went to college and earned a degree in Industrial Marketing. But all that ill equipped me for the rigors of owning my own business and getting a steady flow of customers.

About 21 years ago, I grew tired of working for the big corporation and decided to leave the security of the big corporate job and start a company of my own. I struggled to make it successful. I was barely getting by. I wasn't providing the standard of living for my family that I wanted. I was working all the time and my wife and family were left out.

I knew a lot about selling and when I talked directly to the prospect myself I almost always closed the sale. But I was one person and I couldn't make much money just knocking on doors and selling my products. I was just making a meager living and really dissatisfied with my lot in life. I had made more money working for someone else. What was I going to do, admit failure?

Then one day about 12 years ago, I came to the conclusion that I needed to know a whole lot more about marketing and advertising my business in order to be really successful. I started studying all the top small business marketing masters, current and old time masters, and finally stumbled on to Dan Kennedy. I studied everything I could get my hands on that he wrote. I went to national conferences where I could hear him speak along with others using his methods. I started putting the marketing systems he taught into my business and it miraculously started growing. Then several of my friends wanted me to help them get their businesses to grow because of what they saw happening in my businesses.

I realized there was a significant need in the small businesses around me for someone to help them discover what I had discovered about marketing a small business. That was the stimulus that started my small business marketing training, coaching and consulting company to help struggling businesses succeed.

Do you hear the story there? Does it raise the level of my perceived expertise? You should use stories like this in your business. We have been trained since birth to value stories in our life. It started with fairy tales as a kid. Stories cause us to naturally be more comfortable. If you implement stories in your selling and advertising everywhere you can, I guarantee you will sell more.

The Power of Your Customer Stories

The second story type you should be using is the stories of your customers. Sit down for a moment and conger up some stories that demonstrate how you helped a customer with something that overcame a problem. Or, maybe it is a story that demonstrates a particular way you provide unusual benefit or unusual service rather than what is normally found in your industry.

Whether you are selling directly to a prospect or writing an advertising piece, a customer story is the most powerful way to overcome a potential objection or demonstrate something you do that is important and most customers or prospects don't know about.

I have a great headline I use when I talk about this technique. That headline is:

Why Wayne Tells All His Clients To STOP Answering Objections

Does that get your interest? I'm going to cover the importance of headlines next. But to the topic of stories, most of you answer the objections a customer throws in the way by giving them a whole list of why that objection is not valid or is not as important as the benefits they are going to receive. You just keep selling with more information.

You know you do it. You give them a whole list of facts. That is salesmanship 101. Answer the objection and then trial close, right? Would you like to have a more potent method for answering an objection or making a point? Would you like to have a method that immediately establishes you as the expert?

Telling a short illustrative story is a far better way to answer an objection. Let your customer stories demonstrate the value of your product. Or, use an illustrative story that you have experienced or know about. Stories have 100 times more power than your own words and logic.

If you ever have a one-on-one coaching session with me, you will find that I make most of my points with stories of successes with clients, how clients solved problems or how they demonstrated with their actions the validity of the point I am making.

My well crafted stories are far more interesting; AND you will find yourself believing them more than if I had just out and out told you the strategy or method. It is all subconscious and you may not even realize what is happening. (Well you may now since I have suggested you look for it. I may be revealing too much.)

> # Wayne's Rule
> **The more well crafted stories you tell, the more you sell.**

Specifically designed stories will make you far more believable. You can do it too. Here are a couple of great examples.

My "Red and Green Light Story" That Changes Your Business

I heard this story as a client was giving a testimonial about one of our PowerCircle™ members.

This member owned a carpet cleaning company. One of the members in the room was a customer of this carpet cleaner and told us the following story as her testimonial. I will call her Jane.

Jane had one of those really fancy high-dollar vacuum cleaners that have red and green indicator lights on it. The Red Light comes on to warn the operator that she (in this case) still needed to vacuum more. The Green light tells her she's getting her carpet totally clean.

Several months before, the red light malfunctioned and was staying on all the time. It would never go green to tell her when she had vacuumed enough to be clean.

Then one day, she was planning to have friends in for a special party. So, she had our PowerCircle™ member's company come in and clean her carpets. The carpet really looked beautiful after they left. Just before the party she quickly pulled out the vacuum cleaner to vacuum up some last minute fuzz that someone had tracked in. Immediately the green light came on.

Jane then related, "It turns out the red light hadn't malfunctioned at all. I just wasn't able to get the vacuum to clean the carpet anymore because there was dirt down deep that wouldn't come up."

She did not realize the carpet was dirty because it didn't look that dirty on top. This entire time vacuum cleaner repair was not the problem. She just needed to hire a great carpet cleaning company.

Now, isn't telling that story far more convincing than the carpet cleaning company telling a prospect that carpet collects dirt down deep and vacuuming will not get the job done?

Do yourself a favor. Constantly be on the lookout for this kind of story. Talk to your customers. Find out why they think your services/products were valuable to them. You will discover that many times it is different and probably even better than the reasons you have been quoting, AND you get a story as a bonus.

The "If Only They Knew" Story.

One day I was talking with Richard, a client and owner of a pest control company. He was telling me all about the poor service issues caused by competitors in his industry. He had taught his technicians (and required them to use) some specific methods which eliminate the sources of bugs and critters that get into your house.

Everyone else in his industry just drags a big pump sprayer around the house spraying toxic chemicals inside and outside your home. They are hoping they kill some bugs. Then the homeowner will see dead bugs lying around and think the pest company did something great.

In some applications, Rich's staff does have to spray, at least initially, but can significantly reduce the spraying because of the actions his technician takes around your home on the first visit. When his technicians do have to spray, his company uses environmentally friendly materials that keep you, your children, dogs, cats, parakeet, ferret, kids hamsters or family mountain lion ... (whatever) from getting sick after the technician leaves.

He then explained to me that "if homeowners in New Mexico JUST understood these issues, and what his company did, he could help them become pest/critter free, and in some cases for even less than they are paying now." And his business would grow like wildfire..."if they only knew".

He Needed to Stop "If Only" And Start Telling the Story

I suggested to Richard, that the perfect way to get that across to his prospects was to have his technicians and all his marketing tell "his story" of how he developed these secret methods. Tell them the story of how he was tired of working for one of the big national "bug drown'em" franchise companies and started his own company doing it the right and safe way. When everyone started telling the story, he started closing more customers and his customers started giving him more referrals of friends.

You can do the same. Not in the pest control business of course, but in your own business. Whoa, for a minute there I was afraid that I was going to create a bunch more competition for Rich. But what **is** important is **your** story about **your** business.

One Last Illustration Story

A couple was going out for the evening to celebrate the wife's birthday. They had gotten ready - all dolled up, cat put out, etc.

The taxi arrived, and as the couple walked out of their home, the cat shoots back into the house. Not wanting their often-rowdy cat to have free run of the house while they were out, the husband went back upstairs to chase the cat out.

The wife, not wanting it known that the house would be empty, explained to the taxi driver, "He's just going upstairs to say goodbye to my mother".

A few minutes later, the husband climbed into the cab, and said, "Sorry I took so long, stupid old thing was hiding under the bed and I had to poke her with a mop to get her to come out! She bit and scratched, but I finally did manage to turf her out into the back yard." The cabbie laughed so hard, he hit a parked car.

The message here is the same for your stories. Do not try to get your prospects to respond with dishonest information. Be honest in whatever you do.

I know I should not have to relate this, but sometimes there is a tendency to stretch things a bit too far to try to get someone to respond when we need income. I have made this mistake myself and paid the price. Don't do it. You have plenty of honest stories to use, just start collecting them and writing them down.

Strategy 2:
Use Compelling Headlines
EVERYWHERE

Look into my eyes; follow the pendulum I am swinging. You are getting sleeeepy. You will now believe and understand everything I am about to say.

Headlines ARE your friend. They are the Velcro that grabs your customer's attention and causes them to stick with your marketing device and continue reading.

Headlines and sub-headlines are one of the 3 ingredients that help meet the needs of people that are skimmers and don't read every word. You WILL find that 40-50% of your target market (who are really interested in your product or service) will read just about every word of your sales material. They want all the exciting, even excruciating details.

I know, I know, YOU will not read long copy, right? So you are convinced your customers will refuse to read it also. You have heard from all the advertising media sales people out there that "you must have short distinct copy because that is what works."

Have you ever considered that the reason the media salesperson gives you this advice is because the media they are selling has limited space and limited readership so they have to tell you this garbage to get you to buy the media they are selling?

But then you have probably said to yourself that YOU would not read all that copy.

Wayne's Rule
You are Not Your Customer

I'll bet all of you at one time or another **have** read all the way through someone's long sales letter, dense copy marketing piece or brochure. Why did you do that? You did it because it was of significant interest to you at that time.

You were the right target for that sales letter. That is exactly what you must do with your marketing pieces. You must target it to the right audience that is interested and make it interesting to read. I know that is a lot of "interestings" but I needed to make an important point.

You still are probably not convinced that people will read more than a one page sales letter. I get that all the time. Here's the real problem. You cannot possibly give your prospects all the information they need to know....that allows them to make an informed decision, in a one page flyer or sales letter. There just is not enough room.

One day I was coaching one of my Platinum MasterMind group members who owns a merchant credit card services company. She was telling me that she had written a list of all the reasons that would convince someone they should use a particular service she was providing. That was a very smart exercise. I recommend that process to my clients. She said it took up several pages. Try as she may, she "just couldn't get it all on one page with lots of white space around it." I told her she was exactly right. It needed to be multiple pages. She had worked desperately to get all that information into one page, because that is what she had always been taught.

Often your advertisement or sales letter just has to contain a lot of content in order to give the prospect enough information to make an informed decision. I am sure that media salespeople and other business owners have told you: "They won't read all that stuff". Here lies one of the biggest myths in all of advertising.

Think about it yourself.

You can read a single page of type in about 2-3 minutes. If you were in front of that customer, face to face and toes to toes, would 2-3 minutes of verbal presentation be enough time to get them seriously interested in your product or service?

Of course not! You would want at least 15 – 30 minutes of their time to submit your case. So why do you think it would work in a single page advertisement or sales letter with just a few words and graphics?

Prospects WILL NOT Read
Long Sales Copy IF.....

Okay, okay, I'm going to agree with you. People will not read your multi-page sales letter or dense content display ad, **IF** they are not interested in your product or service, and **IF** your copy is boring and just selling features. They just WILL NOT!

If the prospect is not interested in your product or service that is exactly what you want. You want your prospect universe to self-select their need for or interest in what you sell. If the prospect does have a need or an interest, they will read most everything you give them **IF** it is compelling and interesting.

Let me give you an example.

Let's say you are getting back into playing golf again and are struggling with your drives off the tee box. You can't seem to get those drives to go more than 150 yards and definitely not straight. Then you see a three page article in a golf magazine about this new wiz-bang golf driver club that says it is guaranteed to straighten out your drives and get 275+ yard drives consistently. You know you need something to solve your problem. Will you read the whole three page article to find out the details? You Betcha!

Actually most magazine articles about new products are nothing more than a sales story for the manufacturer. Because the company will have something of value that you just can't do without, you will read the whole article, top to bottom. Come on now, admit it, you read it all because it was interesting and kept you engaged.

Let me go one step further. Let's say you received that same article in the form of a sales letter with pictures of happy men and women driving the ball AND several pages of testimonials. Would you read it then? Of course you would. You have a need and here is a solution and you want to investigate if this solution is for you.

Maybe you love to cook and you have always wanted to learn how to cook French pastries. You get a letter in the mail or you hear about a website that sells a French pastry instruction book and a set of cards that step you through the process. They are also selling a special cookbook that uses this particular cooking method to achieve perfect pastries every time. Would you read a 3, 4, 6, even an 8 page sales letter or a very dense type display add if it were interesting and taught you some things you didn't know? Of course you would.

Interested Prospects Will Read

The point I am making here is that your prospects **WILL** read a full of copy advertisement or multipage sales letter **IF** it is something they want, perceive a need for or that intrigues them. They **WILL** read if it is interesting and engaging. If they are not interested, they definitely will not read it and that is exactly what you want.

But I digress, I want to get back to Headlines. Why do we need them, they just get in the way of having nice square, clean paragraph letter copy, right?

NO, your headline is the grabber that gets your prospect to take time out of their zip zap, run-here-run-there lives. Your prospects are no longer "glass half full or half empty" people. They are "glass running over the brim, flowing down the table and on to the floor" people. The consumer or business buyer is going out of his/her mind busy. You must get them to read what else you have to say if you are going to have any chance of selling them. However, they are not going to read it unless they have a compelling reason that benefits them.

That is where headlines come in. Grabber type headlines give your customers and prospects a "compelling reason" to take interest in what you have to say. If they stop reading the rest of your information because there was nothing that grabbed their attention, you have wasted all your time AND money.

I have used some of them in this book.

Stop the "If Only"
And Start Telling the Story

My Red and Green Light Story
That Changes Your Business

Why Wayne Tells All His Clients
To STOP Answering Objections

Here is the headline to this next point.

Insurance Agent Almost Blows
For Lack Of a Headline

I had an insurance agent client that was sending a letter to his clients to try to sell them additional insurance services. The operative word here is "try" because trying is all he was accomplishing. He was getting no response.

When he asked for help, I started by giving a few recommendations to improve the response on his sales letter. After we took the company letterhead off the top, replaced it with a big interest grabbing headline and his picture, his clients started responding.

He could not believe it. He almost refused to send the letter. "It won't work," he told me. "It doesn't look like an official letter on my letterhead. All of my customers are well-to-do professionals."

In fact, he also knew that his company compliance officer wouldn't approve the letter. He felt there was no use in even trying to get approval. Based on our style letter format and the "Knock Their Socks Off" approach I teach, he reluctantly agreed to test my change. After all, nothing else was working! Low and behold, the compliance officer DID NOT even care. However, the compliance officer did give his advice: "Don't send this. It will just be a waste of your money."

And of course you would listen to a compliance officer's advice because he has so much experience getting customers to respond to marketing, r-i-g-h-t? (I hope you heard the scoffing tone in my voice there.)

If the insurance agent had listened to the compliance officer's "it must look formal" advice, he would have missed a great "Marketing System" discovery.

```
┌─────────────────────────────────────────────┐
│              Wayne's Rule                     │
│          No Headline – No Cash                │
└─────────────────────────────────────────────┘
```

Headlines are the most critical element of any advertising or marketing piece you create. If you miss creating initial interest or fail to get the prospect's attention at the beginning of the device, there will be NO SALE.

You WILL be right; they WILL NOT read all that boring copy.

There is an old time New York advertising man, Bruce Barton that you should study. He said that the "headline is worth, as much as, all the rest of the copy in an advertisement." I recommend (as you start to create an advertising message) you first write out as many headlines as you can conger up. Write at least 20 – 30. Then you can choose the best one of the lot. You might even consider pulling your staff together and get them to brainstorm some headlines. Reward them for the top three in some way. Take your business owner friends out to lunch and get them to help. Or, join one of my Platinum MasterMind groups and get help from other creative entrepreneurs.

Developing good headlines is actually easy once you get started. Be sure you have Dan Kennedy's book: "The Ultimate Sales Letter" available to help you. He has a whole list of headline templates you can use as starters.

This is the most important step you will take in writing copy

Start paying attention to emails you receive, magazine and newspaper articles you read, and sales websites that grab your interest. Then make a list of the best headlines you see. Use that list as idea starters when you get ready to work on your advertisement or marketing piece. At the end of this chapter, you can request a starter list of 150 of some of my favorite headlines ever written in sales copy.

Here are some examples of headlines that a group of business owners in one of my workshops created (in about 15 minutes) from fill in the blank templates found in Dan Kennedy's "Ultimate Sales Letter" book.

See how interesting and thought provoking they are? This group only had a short time to create them. You will find you can do it too, if you just take the time.

How A Simple Hooker Made 1,000 Real Estate Agents Rich

Warning! Coaching May Triple Your Love of Life

Secrets of Cash Flow Your Bank Doesn't Want You To Know

Cosmic Cats Share Secrets of Being Domestic In America

How Saving For Retirement Allowed Me To Start My Dream Business

5 Secrets Of Making Money By Giving Stuff Away

Warning! We Guarantee You'll Never Want To Visit A Used Car Lot Again

You MUST have at least one big interest grabbing headline at the top of every marketing piece you produce. I often use two or three.

Now back to my headline writing process. Take the 20 to 30 headlines you produced that didn't make the top headline for your piece and use some of the next best headlines as sub-headlines in your marketing letter or device.

Remember: NO Headline – No Cash!

Strategy 3:
Every Marketing Device
MUST Have an Offer

Without an offer it is difficult to get people to respond. The offer is what generates response for us. The offer also sets you apart from your competition. Your offer could be any of the following:

- Some special introductory price on one of your products or services,
- Special purchase of a limited number of a product,
- Bundling of products or services for a premium price,
- Group price or rate,
- Free Bonus with purchase,
- Information/book/report with purchase,
- Special gift for just coming in (retail store or restaurant environment),
- Free introductory service (like an auto repair shop that gives a free oil change),
- or free information in the form of a free report, book, CD or DVD, etc in exchange for their name and address or email. '

Don't make the mistake most business owners make of immediately going to discount price as the only offer you can make.

I created a special offer for a pest management company client. It was a limited time offer that when the prospect signed up for the monthly maintenance program they were allowed to choose from one of 3 free gifts: Genuine Leather Ladies Backpack Purse ($29.95 value), Chefmaster 18 Pc BBQ Tool Set ($67.79 value), or a Diamond Cut Ultra 21pc Cutlery and Wood Block Set ($47.97 value). The most expensive one of these cost the pest management company $19. Their annual maintenance program was worth about $500 a year. Is it worth investing $19 to get a $500 sale? Better yet, lifetime average value is about $2,500. Is it worth it then?

My point here? Without an offer you haven't given prospects and customers a reason to respond now, rather than putting off the decision. When a prospect puts off the decision, he often either never gets around to it, or he buys it from the next person who comes along and offers him the product or service.

Wayne's Rule
"No Offer – No Response"

The BIG Mistake

The biggest mistake I find clients making when it comes to offers is burying the offer in the last paragraph of the sales letter or advertisement.

If the offer is really good, you ought to put it right up front to grab interest. Put it in the headline or refer to it in the first couple of paragraphs of your ad or sales letter. If you've done a great job with a powerful offer, you will often get a better response if you make it THE REASON for reading the advertising piece.

If you have ever attended my free 3-Hour "Small Business Customer Vortex Workshop™", you have seen the example direct mail letter I show that Dan Kennedy designed for an insurance agent. It was sent as an introduction letter to new movers in the agent's sales area neighborhoods.

In Dan's redesigned two-page, letter there were actually 3 offers:

- $25 Home Depot gift certificate if they did business,
- $20 cash if the prospect felt the agent wasted their time when she came out, and
- A free houseplant just for making the appointment.

Those are powerful reasons to take a chance on wasting your time, even with an insurance agent. There IS payback. Timeshare companies do this all the time. They give you free vacation hotel rooms or free fun things to do just for coming in and hearing their story. Many people go just to get the free gift and come away with a timeshare they didn't expect to buy. Give your prospects a reason to respond to your marketing piece and you will get far greater response than ever before.

Now then, I am often asked by people I coach, "where do I get good examples of advertising copy and sales letter offers to emulate in my sales pieces." I recommend you start studying the Dan Kennedy Insider's Circle Marketing Letter every month. If you are not already a member, call us at (505) 260-4663, for the forms and our special "Most Incredible Free Gift Ever" offer. Every month there are many examples of good and bad sales copy. Here is a link to find out more about Dan's free gift offer:

www.KnockTheirSocksOffBook.com/dan

Start what copywriters call a "Swipe File". Every time you get a great sales letter or display ad you like, save it in a file to refer back to when you start writing. If the letter has interested you, the same structure may well work on others. I'm going to give you one last "Top Secret" strategy. This is my Top Secret Clearance Only Undercover Agent Strategy. You must not share this with anyone. How would you like to have a great method I use for finding top notch examples of all three of the techniques I have examined in this chapter? You'll find excellent examples of successful sales pieces that work over and over again that you can model. But, you must swear not to tell anyone this strategy. This is just between you and me.

My Clickbank Strategy

Go to the website: Clickbank.com. When you get there you will find this link in very small print at the very top: "Marketplace". Click the link. It will take you to a page that allows you to search through their database for successful internet affiliate programs. That is what Clickbank provides. It manages internet website affiliate programs for other people.

(On the internet an affiliate is someone who recommends your product to their list of prospects and customers and is paid a significant portion of the revenue that new customer generates.)

In the box "Search the Clickbank Marketplace", choose a category (whatever interests you). I chose "health and fitness" for this example. Then in the "sort by" dropdown, choose either "high gravity" or "$ total Sales". Then press the "Go" button.

You will be given a list of the most successful affiliate websites in their system. Look through the sales websites of several of the ones at the top of the list. Read through their web pages and see how they are structured, what elements are included, what they look like, how they are presented.

These companies are very successful at selling products on the web. Go and look at the website they are using to sell the product. You can use these website ads as idea generators and as format suggestions for the marketing pieces you write. You can even use some of the phrases you really like. You will need to change wording to fit your own products, but you get the idea.

You will find powerful models that work and will give you an amazing advantage over your competitors and your business friends. So, don't tell them this secret. It is something I only share with people in my coaching programs.

Okay, just as a recap.

- You are going to incorporate stories in all your sales materials and face to face client presentations.

- You are going to make ample use of headlines and sub-headlines in all your marketing devices to generate better readership and results.

- And last, you are going to make sure no marketing piece goes out without some type of an offer.

This will create greater power in your marketing.

Get My Free Headline List

If you would like a Swipe File list of **150 Of The Best Selling Headlines Ever Written** to get you started, go to my website:

www.KnockTheirSocksOffBook.com/headlines

Join my bi-weekly "Small Business Marketing Prescription Newsletter" and I will send you my free marketing guide of headline examples along with your first newsletter issue.

Chapter Fifteen

You CAN Do It

Now that you have discovered how to change your thinking about small business marketing, you are on the road to a substantial business. A business with a significant bottom line, manufacturing a comfortable lifestyle, and blessing you with the time to do the things in life you enjoy.

You have learned that owning a successful business is more about how you view your business role than about the product itself.

Small businesses do not grow without the business owner going out and promoting the business to its market and developing the two most important assets a business can have: a customer list and a warm prospect list.

However, knowing these things and accomplishing them is the REAL difference between a business owner and an Entrepreneur.

A business owner often is just an employee of the business he owns. The entrepreneur has developed the skills that allow him to sell his business and go out and buy or start a new business and make it the top of its industry in just a couple of years.

Are you going to be an Entrepreneur or an Employee Business Owner?

Remember the story at the beginning of this book about Marvin, the title company owner? He used massive action and smart "Knock Their Socks Off Marketing" to launch his business to stardom quickly in a tough market.

He created a difference in the market for his business. And here is how he answered the "Top of the Heap Question": **"Why should a prospect, or your current customer, take a chance on doing business with you despite all of the other choices they have to spend their money?"**

1. He made himself known to his target prospects by taking massive marketing action.
2. He identified a hole in the marketplace not being filled by the competitors. He paid the real estate agent their commission within 24 hours after the papers were signed. A real estate agent often had to wait weeks to get paid for the real estate they had sold. What they wanted was to be paid immediately.
3. He declared himself the expert on title work and began publishing booklets and information to inform the agents and public about how to protect themselves in a real estate purchase.
4. He kept in constant contact (at least monthly) with his referral base market.

5. He developed a stand-out customer service experience that had his customers and referral partners telling their friends about it.
6. He used targeted selling techniques to close each new client and referral partner.
7. He never took the position that he had to wait his turn in the marketplace to grow his business. He did it immediately.

You CAN create this environment for your business. You CAN grow your business exponentially over the next 12 to 24 months! You do not have to wait! You do not have to HOPE business gets better! It just takes some results oriented marketing education and then some action on your part. I have given you all the tools you need to create that success in your business. You must be different from everyone else if you really want fast exponential growth. It just takes three action steps:

✓ Get off the "Boring Train".
✓ Craft a marketing plan to **"Knock Their Socks Off"**.
✓ Launch "Massive Marketing Action."

Get Into the Information Marketing Business

There is one last mindset change that I would like to recommend. You should become an information marketer.

What do I mean by that?

The truth is this, what your prospects really crave is information that helps them make the right decision and keeps them from being disappointed. Your prospects' lives are filled with disappointment in the products and services they have bought and the companies from whom they have purchased.

201

Prospects (and probably you) constantly feel there is secret insider information they do not know that is costing them money and disappointment. When you become the provider of the information they want, you stand out in a world of mystery where prospects are stumbling around in the dark. The business owner that teaches them how to buy correctly, how to choose the right products or services for their unique situation, that teaches how to ask the right questions before they purchase, will have the prospect's confidence. The prospect will be attracted to that person's business and buy.

So get into the information business. Yes, it does take a little extra work, but the business owners I have talked into taking this action are finding their businesses growing faster than ever before. There is so much you know about your business, products and industry that prospects do not know. The truth is you may not even be aware of how much your prospects don't know. Just give them the information and they will reward you.

Yes, all that I have shared with you in this book takes time and effort. But these are the elements that make a business stand out in an advertising saturated world around you. Just take it one step at a time. Add one element this month and another next month and so on. You will end up with an automated system bringing in customers like never before.

I am often asked, "Wayne, all this is great, but what is the ONE thing that I can implement that will get me 25 more new customers this month." The truth is? I am not a miracle worker. I do not have ONE WAY you can get 25 more customers this month. But, I do know 25 WAYS to automatically get 1 or 2 or 3 new customer this month. Set a number of these in place to automatically work for you every month and you WILL have the amazing, exponential growth you want for your business.

It just takes a little work and one step at a time. The result? In 12 months, 18 months or 24 months you will be getting those 25 new customers each and every month and all their lifetime value making you wealthy, giving you the time to spend with your family and completing your bucket list.

I know it is working for me and my clients. I know it can work for you.

Just Do It NOW!

If you need help customizing any of the strategies in this book for your business, call my office at (505) 260-4663 and book a 30 minute telephone conference in my busy schedule for a special intro investment of only $97. We will discuss your needs to see how I can help you expand and grow your business with "Knock Their Socks Off Marketing" systems. If we decide to work together, I will apply this initial investment to your consulting or coaching program. You may also find out more about our services at: www.MarketingStrategiesRx.com.

About The Author

As the owner of 3 active businesses in New Mexico and the builder of 9 different businesses in the last 21 years, J Wayne Story has studied all the top minds in small business marketing and advertising. That study has led him to realize that the most effective marketing and advertising strategies are not those that are most popular and most often taught to small business owners.

Wayne is a coach and consultant to many small and medium sized business owners in the Southwest and across the United States. He helps business owners apply and implement non-traditional principles of small business direct response marketing. As a result, he has been dubbed the Dr. of Direct Results Marketing.

Wayne frequently speaks to small business owners and sales professionals about results oriented marketing topics and the effect of the slow economy on business owners. If you would like to have him speak to your organization, call his office at (505) 260-4663, or write to Direct Marketing Strategies Rx Ltd, 1558 Stephanie Rd, Suite 101, Rio Rancho, NM 87124, to reserve a slot on his busy schedule.

Wayne tenaciously earned an Industrial Marketing degree from the University of Houston in 1975 after 9 years in night school. He never allowed a lack of money or scholarships prevent him from his goal. He invested 23 years in corporate sales and sales management for several Fortune 500 companies selling technology products and services. He was also an insider with Robert Kiyosaki (Rich Dad Poor Dad) for 6 years and attended his by invitation only product and book launch dinner parties in Paradise Valley, Arizona.

Wayne has been certified as an Independent Business Advisor, specializing in small business marketing, by the Glazer-Kennedy Insider's Circle, Chicago, Illinois. He also invests in the community as a Big Brother for Big Brothers Big Sisters and is the Board President of KeepItQuerque, the Albuquerque Independent Business Alliance.

For fun, Wayne is a Commercial Hot Air Balloon pilot and flies his 7 story tall balloon Santa Fe Sunrise at balloon rallies and events all over North America.

In 1992, Wayne was tired of his 8-5, working for companies that did not appreciate him, corporate sales management job. He started creating businesses over the next 21 years in the mortgage industry, commercial leasing industry, invention marketing industry, retail website catalog industry, real estate investments and small business coaching and consulting.

All of his sales experience and formal business education failed miserably to prepare Wayne for running and growing a small business. By studying the marketing greats and "trial and error implementation" of many of the proven advertising and marketing on steroids strategies and tactics, he brings a unique ability to present "strategies that I have used myself that work", not just theory.

Special Offer

Free 2-CD Set - $79 Value
"7 Quickest Ways To Get More Customers"

I have compiled a list of the 7 fastest marketing systems to get you more customers. It is a 2-CD set you can take with you and review in your car as you drive to your next appointment or convert to MP3 and listen on the go.

You will learn my best strategies like:

➢ The secret to getting your prospects to respond faster.

➢ The strategy I use to get a higher price for my products and services than my competitors and as a result more profit.

➢ The secret phrase to say when you get to the point of asking for the sale that will double or triple your close ratio in front of your customer.

➢ Examples of how these strategies are used in all different types of businesses but especially in the local-centric business.

➢ One strategy missed by almost all restaurants that is stunting your growth and will catapult your revenues even if you are not a restaurant.

➢ How you can get customers to prefer your business over all your competitors for the rest of your business life. This one can be transferred to any business you will own in the future.

To get your free copy of "The 7 Quickest Ways to Get More Customers" go to this website page and we will mail it to you for just the shipping and handling of $7.95.

www.KnockTheirSocksOffBook.com/CD

Made in the USA
San Bernardino, CA
30 March 2013